A YOUNG
SOFT
BALL
PLAYER'S GUIDE
TO FIELDING AND
DEFENSE

DON OSTER & JACQUE HUNTER

THE LYONS PRESS
GUILFORD, CONNECTICUT
An imprint of The Globe Pequot Press

To buy books in quantity for corporate use
or incentives, call **(800) 962–0973**
or e-mail **premiums@GlobePequot.com.**

The Lyons Press is an imprint of The Globe Pequot Press.

All interior photos by the authors.

10 9 8 7 6 5 4 3 2 1

Printed in the United States of America

ISBN 978-1-59921-023-0

Library of Congress Cataloging-in-Publication Data is available.

CONTENTS

ACKNOWLEDGMENTS

We want to take this opportunity to thank all our former players, for their hard work, and their parents, for the support they provided during our years of coaching. We also want to recognize the contributions of all our former assistant coaches, especially Don Sisloff and Dennis Richardson.

Robert Holmes, former superintendent of the New Albany-Floyd County Consolidated School Corporation in Indiana, had a vision of the future when he started promoting athletic opportunities for young women more than thirty years ago.

Thanks also to the New Albany, Indiana, High School Athletic Department and to Don Unruh, the athletic director, for use of the field where we took photos for this book. Finally, thanks to Chelsea Alldaffer, Kala Prater, and Stephanie Cotner, who assisted in the photo process.

INTRODUCTION

Team defense wins ball games. It's that simple. In the higher levels of fast pitch softball, pitchers can and usually do dominate games. Close games decided by one or two runs are the norm. Pitching effectiveness is the cornerstone of any defense, and it is rare for a pitcher to strike out all of the opposing team's batters. Obviously, opponents must score to win. The outcome of most games hinges on the ability of the defense to retire the batters who put the ball in play and any runners who reach base.

Playing "small ball" is a term to describe teams who attempt to scratch out runs by putting pressure on a defense. They do this by concentrating on making contact to put the ball in play. They are very aggressive on the base paths as runners attempt to steal bases, and they bunt often to reach base or advance runners. Fast pitch softball is tailor-made made for teams to take this approach. A team that can't meet the challenge and make the plays will not be very successful.

It is a team game. And having an effective defense depends on the ability of each player at each position to make a play when the opportunity arises. Learning to play defense is not the most simple or exciting facet of the game—but it is most vital to winning ball games. This book is about learning how to make a contribution to team success by being a good defensive player.

Fundamentals of fielding and throwing are covered in the first four chapters. These basic skills apply to play at all positions. You will learn how to field fly balls, field ground balls, and make good accurate throws. You can't overpractice these fundamentals. Drills to develop and improve your fielding and throwing are included in each chapter. The goal is to practice until fielding and making good throws becomes automatic. It is important to develop these skills early in your playing career. They will apply as long as you play the game.

Next we cover how to play defense at each position. Fielding and throwing are important parts of playing any position well, but there is much more to being a good defensive player. You must think ahead and know where to make a play when the ball comes your way. This is called "having your head in the game." Smart defenses seldom commit errors that cost the team runs. Players at each position have a specific job to do, depending on the game situation. These jobs are outlined for each position in chapters six through twelve. The following chapters describe a game-winning team defense and mistakes for fielders to avoid. Having fun is what the game is all about, but the final chapter outlines serious opportunities available to the player who develops into a complete player.

FIELDING BASICS

We begin this book with a chapter on basics that apply to all fielders—with the exception, at times, being the catcher. These basic principles include being ready to field, proper use of the glove, footwork, moving to field balls, and getting the feet in position to make a throw. They apply when fielding throws, fly balls, line drives, and grounders. Players who learn these basic techniques and practice them until they become automatic responses can become excellent fielders.

CATCHING THE BALL

Glove Position

Proper glove position when catching a ball is the first principle of fielding. Many young players have difficulty getting it right, but the rule is simple. Catch the ball above the waist with the fingers pointed up, and catch balls below the waist with the fingers pointed down. This rule is absolute and applies to catching ground balls, fly balls, throws, and line drives.

Many young players attempt to catch high throws with their fingers pointed down. It is also common to see them try to trap or smother a low throw with their fingers pointed up. Either of these methods is incorrect and makes it almost impossible to make a good catch. Not practicing the "fingers up, fingers down" rule has been the reason why many young players are injured when trying to catch a ball. Having the glove in the proper position will feel like the natural way to catch the ball. You can let the ball come to you and catch it more easily as it arrives.

Use Both Hands

One-handed catches may look flashy or fancy, but one-armed wonders make a lot of errors. There are times when a one-handed catch may be necessary because

Fingers up to catch above the waist

Fingers down to catch below the waist

Make two-handed catches whenever possible.

the ball is almost out of reach. But you should always use two hands to make a catch when you can reach the ball. As the ball reaches the glove, secure it with your bare hand. This is the surest way to make a catch—and your hand is already on the ball, ready to grip it and pull it from the glove to make a throw.

Soft Hands

If you receive the ball when your glove hand is stiff or rigid, the ball will likely try to pop back out of your glove. Good fielders are described as having "soft

4

hands." This means that the player's glove hand gives slightly as she catches the ball. This slight movement or "give" helps secure the ball in the glove, even when the ball is hit or thrown very hard. The opposite of soft hands is "brick hands." Imagine how difficult a ball would be to catch if a glove was as hard as a brick.

Practice

Being skilled at catching a ball is the first vital step toward becoming a good fielder. And catching is almost impossible to overpractice. Learning to catch is also one of the simplest of all practice drills. Find a teammate, friend, or grown-up to play catch with you. As you throw and then catch the ball, practice the fingers up, fingers down rule and catch with both hands. Also start to develop soft hands with each catch.

One thing to try at the outset to see if you are developing soft hands is to play catch bare-handed with tennis balls. Tennis balls rebound quickly if they meet a rigid surface. If you can't find someone to play catch with, find a wall and practice by yourself with tennis balls. If you throw the ball and it hits the wall first, the ball will usually return below your waist. Catch it fingers down. The ball thrown to hit the ground first will rebound above your waist. Get it with your fingers up.

FOOTWORK

Good footwork is the foundation of good fielding. Unless a thrown or batted ball is coming directly at you, your feet should move first. You must move your feet to get your body into position in front of the ball so you can field it cleanly. Fielders who try to field a ball reaching to the side when they have time to get in front of a ball make a lot of errors. There will be situations when you must reach to make a play, but you should try to get your body in front of the ball if at all possible.

Your footwork should enable you to maintain good balance as you field the ball. No matter which direction you must go, you want to be smooth and under control as you move toward the ball to field it. Specific examples of footwork used to get to the ball will be covered in following chapters on fielding ground balls, fielding fly balls, and making throws.

Ready to Make a Throw

When the ball is fielded, the feet should be in a position to initiate a throw. A right-hander's plant foot is the right foot; her lead foot is her left foot. The lefty's plant foot is her left foot; the lead foot is her right foot. As the ball is received, the fielder should be well balanced with the lead foot slightly in front of the plant foot. In this

Foot position when fielding the ball

position, the feet are in the basic position to quickly make the shuffle step and throw. Throwing mechanics will be covered in chapter four.

Practice your footwork when you are playing catch. Always move to get in front of the ball, stay balanced, and have your feet ready to make a step and throw to return the ball to your partner.

THE READY POSITION

One final constant for fielders is getting the body into position to field a ball. Get into this ready position any time you are practicing by playing catch or fielding balls.

This is your basic body position to be ready to field, and it should become automatic.

When a pitch is released in a game, the ready position is the same for all fielders except the pitcher and catcher. The pitcher should get into a ready position after her follow-through because she becomes a fielder as soon as the pitch is released. Before each pitch you should be loose and relaxed. If you are tense or tight, you won't be ready to move quickly to a ball hit toward your position. Set your feet about shoulder width apart. Bend slightly at your waist, keeping your back straight. Hold your glove and bare hand in front of your body,

The ready position

separated at the level of your knees. Focus your eyes on the pitcher.

When the pitcher is in the windup, shift your weight onto the balls of your feet. This weight shift will cause your knees to bend and move your body slightly forward and lower to the ground. The weight shift gets you on your toes, ready to move as necessary. Keep your eyes on the ball as the pitch approaches the batter.

THINGS TO REMEMBER

1. Fingers up, fingers down.
2. Catch with soft hands.
3. Catch with both hands.
4. Stay smooth and balanced.
5. Get in front of the ball.
6. Stay balanced, with feet set ready to throw.
7. Practice getting into the ready position.

FIELDING GROUND BALLS

This chapter deals with the techniques to use when fielding ground balls. Again, with the exception of the catcher, these techniques are the same for all fielders. Much of the skill in fielding ground balls has to do with proper body position and footwork. Good fielders seem to always get these elements right. Fielding always starts with the fielder in the ready position you learned in chapter one.

No matter what the game situation, following are the fundamentals of fielding ground balls.

SEE THE BALL

In your ready position, you must focus on the ball as it leaves the pitcher's hand. See the ball approach the batter, then see the ball leave the bat as it is contacted. If the ball is hit your way, your feet should start to move you toward the path of the ball.

GET TO THE BALL: STAY LOW

Get in front of the ball as fast as you can. Stay low, smooth, and balanced as you move into the path of the ball. Keep your glove low to the ground as the ball approaches. The expression is to "get your glove dirty." Staying low and getting your glove down will prevent the ball from bouncing under your glove. It is easier to bring the glove up to catch a grounder than to go down on one.

PLAY THE BALL

Field the ball as you reach it. Sometimes you will get a good high bounce, called a "Sunday hop," that is easy to field. But most of the time the bounces are not very easy. Back up to field a ball only if it is over your head. Never try to back up or move your body to get a good bounce. This cardinal sin is called "letting the ball play you." Unless it's a real slow roller, which we will cover later, learn to stand your ground and play the hop you get. Letting the ball play you is a quick road to a lot of errors.

Basic Fielding Position

When you have gotten in front of the ball, you should be in a basic fielding position as it arrives. This position is similar to the ready position. You are balanced on the balls of your feet and your eyes are focused on the ball. Now your glove and body are lower and your bare hand is ready to secure the ball as soon as it gets to your glove.

Be ready for a bad hop as the ball approaches.

As the ball hops toward you, you must be ready for a bad bounce. The ball may hit a pebble, a clump of dirt, or another irregularity on the field and hop high, skid, or bounce to the side. These bad hops can happen even on well-groomed fields—meaning you must always be ready to react. In your low basic fielding position, your hands must be ahead of you, relaxed, and ready to move with the ball. Be assured, you will not field all of the grounders that take a bad hop. But being in front of the ball gives you an opportunity to knock down or stop the ball even if you can't field it cleanly. Keeping the ball near you, where you might make a play, can keep any runners from advancing.

When you field the ball, your lead foot should be placed slightly ahead of your plant foot. This foot placement is the first step in starting the throwing motion, as you will learn in chapter four.

RECEIVING THE BALL

When you catch the ball in your glove, first cover it with your bare hand. Grip the ball with the fingers of your bare hand as you smoothly bring both hands to your waist. This movement of hands to the waist is the second step in starting the throwing motion explained in chapter four.

Balls Hit at Your Position

If they are not slow rollers, balls hit right at you should be easy routine plays. From your ready position you can quickly get into the basic fielding position. Then stay low and play the ball with soft hands as it comes to you. Receive the ball with your feet set to initiate a throw.

Balls Hit to the Side

In your ready position your eyes are focused on the ball as it leaves the bat. If the ball is coming toward your position, you have a judgment call to make. The decision is simple if the ball is hit directly at you. But if the ball is hit to the side, you must quickly decide how to play it. By judging the direction and speed of the grounder you will determine the footwork needed to make the play.

For example, if the ball is hit slightly to your left, your first step is slightly out with your left foot. The movement to get to the ball is two or three sideways shuffle steps. If the ball is slightly to your right, the first step is out with the right foot; then take the sideways shuffle steps to get in front of the ball and into the fielding position. Based on the speed and direction of the grounder, you could make the play using shuffle steps.

But all ground balls hit to the side will not be reachable using shuffle steps. Again, how you get to

Ball to left, turn out the left foot

Crossover step with the right leg

the ball hit far to the side will be up to your judgment. If a ground ball looks to be out of shuffle step range, you must use another technique to quickly get to the ball. If the ball is far to your left, the first step is on your left foot with your toe turned out. This gets your body turned to the side to get you started on the next step. The second step is a "crossover" step. It is the quickest way to get to a ball that is nearly out of reach. You make this step by crossing your right leg over and in front of your left leg. As you cross your right leg over, push with your left foot and take a long stride with your right leg. You are now in stride to go get the ball. To reach the ball, you may need to really stretch out. As you receive the ball, set your plant foot and get your balance before trying to make a throw.

A grounder hit far to the right will also require a crossover step. The first step is with the right foot with the toe turned out. The crossover step is made by crossing the left leg over and in front of your right leg. As you cross over, push off with the right foot and take a long stride with your left leg. You may need to make a backhand catch of this ball. To get into position to make a throw, turn your body to point your lead shoulder toward the target as you set your plant foot. Be sure you are balanced before trying to throw.

Ball to the right, turn out the right foot

Crossover step with the left leg

Make backhand catch

The footwork for a left-handed player in these examples is the same as a right-handed player. However, a lefty may need to stretch for a ball hit far to the right and backhand a ball hit far to the left.

Slow Rollers

This applies to infield slow rollers. When you see a "dribbler" leave the bat, instantly charge it as fast as you can. Stay low, smooth, and balanced but get to the ball quickly. Scoop the ball up in your hands, set your feet, and quickly make the throw. Waiting for a slow roller to come to you gives a runner a good chance of reaching base safely.

GROUND BALLS IN THE OUTFIELD

The techniques for fielding ground balls in the infield and outfield are basically the same. Some of the major differences exist because of the space an outfielder must cover. A hard-hit ground ball may be traveling directly at the outfielder's position, and the player may be able to field it the same as an infielder. A ball that is not hit hard should be charged by the outfielder and returned quickly to the infield to prevent any runners from advancing.

Hard-hit balls to either side of an outfielder will require frequent use of a crossover step. But because of the space in the outfield, the player may also need to circle to get in front of a ball, or run back to chase down a ball that rolls past her position.

Some coaches teach young outfielders to drop to one knee in front of a ground ball when fielding. The intent here is that the knee is supposed to block the ball. Do this only if your coach insists. Dropping to a knee takes you out of a good fielding position and it requires more time to get set to make a throw. The delay in making the throw can allow runners to advance.

PRACTICE DRILLS

When doing these practice drills with a ball, find a place with a smooth surface. As you go through the drills, you don't need the variable of bad bounces to be a factor. Some of the drills will require a partner, but there are also ways to practice by yourself.

Verbal Position Drill

You need a partner for this drill. It is meant to help you develop good footwork. Get into the ready position. Your partner will give instructions such as, "At you," "Right," or "Left!" Move the direction indicated first with side shuffle steps and get into the basic fielding position. Fake fielding the ball and making a throw. Then have your partner call "Far right," or "Far left," and practice making the crossover step. Again, complete the drill by faking a catch and throw. Do twenty repetitions.

Shuffle Drill

Do this drill without a glove. The fielder and partner set up facing each other about 6 feet apart. The fielder should get into the basic ground ball fielding position. The partner rolls a ball to the side of the fielder who picks it up with both hands and returns it with a soft underhand toss. The partner rolls the ball first right, then left, then back right in quick succession as the fielder makes the moves and returns the ball. Each of the right-left rolls should be two or three shuffle steps to the side of the fielder. Do two sets of ten of this drill.

Toss, Catch, and Throw

This drill also requires two people: the tosser and the fielder. This drill is similar to the verbal position drill except that now ground balls are tossed to be fielded. Set up about 20 feet apart. The fielder should be in the ready position. The tosser should roll ground balls at or to either side of the fielder, who fields and makes a return throw. When doing this drill, the fielder should concentrate on footwork and proper fielding form. Twenty repetitions should be enough of this drill.

Pepper

This drill is as old as baseball and softball. A batter and one or more fielders face each other at a distance of about 20 feet. All fielders should be in the ready position. A fielder makes a soft underhand toss to the batter who punches the ball back toward the fielder(s).

This is good practice because the batted ball can go anywhere and will provide fielders with many different bounces to field.

Live Ground Balls

None of the drills we've described may be a part of your team's practice routine. If not, practice them on your own. They are valuable in helping you develop sound defensive skills. However, there is no substitute for fielding live batted ground balls. This will definitely be a part of team practice and an opportunity to sharpen your skills. Team infield and outfield practice or pregame warm-ups with batted balls are as close to actual game situations as you can get.

There are endless games that can be made out of ground ball fielding practice. Count how many good plays can be made in a row. Eliminate fielders who make errors until there is a winner. Competition can make it fun to sharpen fielding skills.

THINGS TO REMEMBER

1. Focus on the ball from the bat to your glove.
2. Develop and practice good footwork.
3. Get in front of the ball as quickly as possible.
4. Play the ball; don't let it play you.
5. Field with soft hands.

6. Have your feet in position to initiate a throw as you field.

7. Practice, practice, practice.

3

FIELDING POP-UPS AND FLY BALLS

The fundamentals for fielding pop-ups and fly balls are similar to those for fielding ground balls. Fielders start in the ready position, use the same footwork to get to the ball quickly, make plays with the ball in front of the body, catch with soft hands, and receive the ball with the feet in position to initiate a throw.

A few rules need to be stated at the outset of this chapter. Teammates are on the field with you, and a fly ball or pop-up may be hit anywhere. The fielder who has the ball judged and can make the play must call off all other fielders by yelling in a loud voice, "I've got it!" This will avoid a possible collision and injury. It is good

Field fly balls at or above shoulder level.

to call out more than once if time permits. The fielder who calls for the ball must then make the catch. "I've got it, No, you take it" is not smart play.

The second rule: It is always easier to move in to make a catch than it is to go back to make one. This establishes a priority of who should call for the ball and make the play when the ball is hit between two fielders.

BASIC FIELDING POSITION

When you can get to a fly ball or pop-up, you should be in a basic fielding position to make the catch. You should have your weight on the balls of your feet with your feet spread about shoulder width apart. Your lead foot will be slightly ahead of your plant foot to help get a throw off quickly. Your hands should be at shoulder height with your bare hand ready to secure the ball as soon as it enters your glove.

You should use this basic position anytime you are making a routine play. But all balls hit into the air can't be caught easily. Infielders will at times need to hustle to get to pop-ups, and outfielders may need to run full out to reach fly balls. In these cases, a catch below the waist with fingers down may be necessary. Hard-to-reach balls to the side may only be caught with a stretch to one side or backhand catch to the other side. When a running catch is made, the fielder should receive the ball, square the body, and be sure to get on balance with both feet in position before trying to throw.

JUDGING FLY BALLS AND POP-UPS

It is very hard to teach absolute rules about how to judge balls hit into the air. Lots of practice at catching fly balls and pop-ups reinforced by experience are the best ways to learn. However, there are some principles to get you started.

When a ball leaves the bat there are three variables. The first is easy to see: it is the direction the ball is traveling in. As a fielder, you know to start moving in that direction. The second variable is the angle of ascent as it leaves the bat. From seeing the angle you get an idea as to how far the ball may travel. A ball that goes almost straight up will be a pop-up, probably into the infield. A less-sharp angle will allow the ball to travel farther, possibly well into the outfield. The third variable is how hard the ball is hit. This final factor of velocity is the one that makes judging fly balls a difficult task.

Pop-ups are relatively easy. The ball goes up at a sharp angle, reaches its apex, and comes down at about the same angle. If it is hit hard, it will go high in the air, giving the fielder time to move quickly to the spot where she thinks the ball will come down. Then she can adjust to be under the ball to make the catch. Short, lightly hit pop-ups are usually a run and catch-as-catch-can on the run affair. Pop-ups near the plate that will be handled by the catcher are another matter that will be covered in chapter eleven.

Fly balls to the outfield are more difficult. You can see the direction and if the ball is not hit toward you, move in that direction as quickly as possible. As you watch the ball rise over the infield, run at an angle to intercept the ball as it comes down. Obviously, a ball with a high trajectory gives the fielder more time to track it down. Hard-hit balls with a lower trajectory are harder to reach. Never take your eyes off the ball. Stay smooth and under control as you track toward the ball.

Other Factors

Sun and wind are additional factors that can cause difficulty when making plays on fly balls. When a fielder takes her position, she should note the direction and angle of the sun. On a bright sunny day, an outfielder may wear sunglasses. Wearing a cap or visor helps, but a fielder may need to shade her eyes from the sun with her throwing hand when making a fly ball catch.

Wind can affect the ball in flight. Pay attention to the wind direction and make allowances for it when judging fly balls. Strong crosswinds can cause the ball to fade to the side. Wind blowing in toward home plate can slow down fly balls, and wind blowing out away from home plate can cause balls to carry farther than normal. Pop-ups will be blown to the downwind side; the fielder must be ready to move to the ball as it descends.

Check out the height, glare, and intensity of the lights when playing a night game. It may be necessary to use your hand to shield your eyes from light glare when fielding a fly or pop-up. All field lighting systems are not well done. Note if the area around your position is lit evenly. A ball traveling from a brightly lit area into a darker area can be difficult to see well.

Balls Hit at You

When a ball leaves the bat in the air, you can tell if it is hit in your direction. This is a hard ball to judge. Many young fielders make the terrible mistake of instantly starting to move toward the ball. A fielder should hesitate for an instant then move to make a catch once she has judged the height and speed of the ball. From an outfielder's perspective, there is an instant when a short looping fly that will barely get out of the infield will almost look exactly the same as a smash that might go to the fence. Move in quickly on the short fly; move back to catch the long ball. Nothing is worse for a fielder than to move in on a ball that goes over her head.

Going Back to Make a Catch

The technique for going back to catch a fly ball or pop-up is the same for both infielders and outfielders. Always keep your eyes focused on the ball. For a ball hit to the right, turn your body to the right and look over your left shoulder as you track toward the ball. If the ball is hit to your left, turn your body to the left and look over your right shoulder. Run on the balls of your feet, be fast, and stay smooth as you stride.

A ball hit straight back over your head is the toughest play to make. You must turn and run, looking back

Running catch over the right shoulder

at the ball. If you are right-handed, try to look over your right shoulder. When you get to the ball you won't need to make a backhand catch A lefty should turn and look over her left shoulder for the same reason. In no case should a fielder try to back up to make a play on a ball hit over her head.

Do not charge back at full speed to a fly ball near the fence. The outfield may have a wide strip of gravel near the fence called a "warning track." If the field has a warning track, you will hear the crunch of gravel under your feet. This means you are nearing the fence and a potential crash and injury. You must be extra careful if there is no warning track and you know you're getting near the fence. Reach out with your bare hand to find the fence and stop before you make contact with your body. Keep your eyes on the ball and make the catch.

CATCHES *NOT* TO MAKE

Shoestring catches Making a running catch on a ball just before it hits the ground is very risky. Make it and it's flashy; miss it and you can give the batter-runner one or two extra bases. It is better to slow up and play the ball on the bounce.

Diving catches Diving catches are risky and potentially dangerous. If you must try, go in under as much control as possible.

Basket catches This is the term for catching fly balls at the waist with the palms of both hands pointing up. It is showy and is not the recommended way to field fly balls. Stay with the fundamentals.

One-hand catches Make one-handed catches only when it is the only way to reach the ball. Two-handed catches are more reliable and throws can be made quicker.

PRACTICE DRILLS

As we have mentioned before, there is no shortcut to learning how to judge fly balls. Practice and experience are the best teachers. Like fielding ground balls, it is hard to overpractice. When you practice catching fly balls, do it under all kinds of sun, wind, and sky conditions. Position yourself and a tosser or batter so you are facing the sun. When there is a strong wind, move so the wind will be blowing from different directions on the ball in flight. Also practice under the lights to prepare for night games.

Verbal Footwork Drill

You need a fielder and a helper for this drill. The fielder gets in the ready position and the helper shouts direction, such as left, back, in, and right. The fielder goes through all the moves to field and throw the ball. When you are doing this drill, concentrate on form and footwork. Do twenty repetitions per session.

Toss Drill

This drill is similar to the verbal drill with one player tossing fly balls for the fielder. The fielder and tosser should be about 20 feet apart. The fielder is set up in the ready position and the tosser throws fly balls to the right, left, in back, and short of the fielder. The fielder makes the catches and makes a soft return throw to the tosser. The tosser and fielder should trade duties after about two dozen repetitions. As you become proficient, the tosser and fielder should move farther apart and the tosser should throw the ball to make the plays more difficult. You can't overdo this drill.

Live Fielding and Throwing

Team practices will include catching live batted fly balls. This is where a fielder faces the reality of balls hit in any direction. In other drills, the tosser can control the length and arc of each toss. When fielding live batted balls, anything can happen. It is the nearest thing to game conditions and the best way to learn to field fly balls.

THINGS TO REMEMBER

1. Be aware of wind, sun, and light conditions.
2. Get to the ball as quickly as possible.
3. Use the basic fly ball fielding position to make a catch whenever possible.
4. Square your shoulders and be balanced before starting to make a throw.
5. Practice, practice, practice.

4

MAKING ACCURATE THROWS

To be a complete defensive player, you must be able
to consistently make accurate throws. Most times
when you field a ball, you make a throw to complete a
play. We have already talked about receiving the ball
when you field, and about getting your feet set to
throw. In this chapter, we will outline in detail the mechanics of throwing.

The throwing motion should be continuous and
smooth. But the motion is not as simple as it seems because throwing requires you to use your entire body
properly, not just your arm. The way you coordinate all

of the moving parts to make a throw is called the "me-chanics of throwing."

When we talk about the throwing motion, we will be talking about the plant foot and the lead foot. These have been mentioned before, but to review again: A right-hander plants on the right foot to throw, and the left foot is the lead foot; the left-hander plants on the left foot, with her right being the lead foot. In this chapter, we will be talking mainly about making an overhand throw. This is the most accurate type of throw and the one most commonly used in ball games.

Make the catch.

Receive the ball and shuffle step.

THE MECHANICS OF THROWING

The first step in making a throw starts immediately after you field the ball. In the previous chapters on fielding, you caught the ball in your glove and secured it with your throwing hand. Next, you received the ball by moving both hands to waist level and back near your body on the side of your throwing arm. As you receive the ball, your lead foot should be slightly ahead of your plant foot. Square your body by pointing your front shoulder toward the target. In this position you should be balanced on both feet, your head should be still, and your eyes should be focused on the target.

37

The Grip

As you receive the ball, grip it with your throwing hand. Try to use a two-finger grip, between your thumb and your index and middle fingers. However, at a younger age, your hand may be too small to use this grip. Use three fingers or all four fingers if necessary.

It is important that your grip feels comfortable and gives you good control of the ball when it is released. As you grow older, change your grip as soon as your hand size allows, gripping the ball with two fingers. With a smaller hand size, the ball will be touching the palm of the hand when it is gripped. Again, if your hand size allows, grip the ball slightly out in the fingers, away from the palm. This grip will allow you to make harder throws.

Shuffle and Stride

You are now in a balanced, set position ready to start the throw. Gripping the ball in your throwing hand, reach back with your throwing arm. At the same time, shift your weight to your plant foot by taking a short shuffle step toward the target with your plant foot. Next push off with your plant foot and stride toward the target with your lead foot. Raise your glove hand toward the target as you bring your arm forward to make the throw.

There is no magic distance in which to make either the shuffle step or the stride. How far either movement

Stride and reach back.

is made depends on your body size and the length of your legs. Both moves must be comfortable and must not affect your balance. The shuffle step, arm movement, stride, and throw should be a smooth continuous motion. Throughout this motion, your head should remain still with your eyes focused on the target.

The Release

As your arm comes over the top to make the throw, your elbow actually leads your arm through the throw. Your front shoulder opens up and your glove hand and arm drop down toward your side. Your wrist is slightly open as your arm comes forward. When you release the ball, you

39

Release the throw.

will snap it downward with a smooth quick motion, letting the ball roll off the tips of your fingers. Your release point will determine how high or low your throw will go.

The Follow-Through

After you release the throw, let your throwing arm continue in a smooth arc toward the ground. Let your plant foot and leg swing around so you finish with your body facing the target.

INFIELDER THROWS

A big part of an infielder's job is fielding balls and throwing out runners. An infielder needs to get to a ground

Follow through.

ball quickly, field it, and throw out the runner. Good infielders can field the ball and get it on its way quickly. They are described as having good hands and a quick release. But good throwing mechanics must not be sacrificed to get rid of the ball quickly. The coordination of hand, arm, and footwork must be done smoothly and quickly to get the desired result.

In the early age groups, infielders may need to fully extend the arm and take a long stride to make infield throws. As players grow stronger in later years, the throws can be made with less effort, but the quick release will always be important.

Infielders may also make short tosses on some

plays. Distance is the key. The throw between the second baseman and shortstop to make a force play at second base may be a short overhand snap throw. If these two infielders are very close, the throw may be a soft underhand toss. Catchers also make snap throws, which will be described when we cover that position in a later chapter.

Cutoff Play

The longest throw an infielder will make is during a cutoff play. A cutoff play occurs when there is any fair hit deep into the outfield, or there is a long fly ball hit with a runner(s) on base. As the outfielder goes for the ball, the shortstop or second baseman goes into the outfield as a "cutoff" to take a throw from the outfielder and make a relay throw to a base. This will be repeated later, but the shortstop is the cutoff on balls hit to left and center fields; the second baseman handles balls hit toward right field. When the infielder takes the throw and makes the relay to a base or home plate, this will likely be her longest throw.

OUTFIELD THROWS

Most outfield throws are longer, requiring the player to fully extend her arm back. For these longer throws the plant, shuffle step, and stride will be more powerful.

When making a throw to the cutoff, the outfielder should aim the ball at the cutoff player's chest. There is an advanced method of making the longer throw from the outfield following a fly ball catch. The outfielder sets up a couple of steps back from where the ball comes down, catches it moving toward the target, strides, and makes the throw. This running into the throw should be attempted only after a fielder has developed very good fielding and throwing skills.

Finally, outfield throws should not be thrown with a high arc. If the outfielder can't get the ball to a base on a line, it is best to keep the throw down so it reaches the base on a hop. The low throw or one on a hop gets to the base quicker than a rainbow throw; it is also easier for the infielder covering the base to catch the ball and make a tag.

OTIIER TYPES OF THROWS

There are a couple of other throws that fielders may make—but only after practicing them and gaining confidence in their accuracy. The same principles of footwork and balance apply when making these throws. An infielder may make a sidearm throw to get a throw off quickly. This is a circumstance when an infielder gets a ground ball and feels there isn't enough time to straighten up, reach back, and throw overhand. When the fielder receives the ball, the body position and footwork are the same as an overhand throw, but the throwing arm extension is shorter and the delivery and release are at or near the level of the waist.

The other type of throw is underhand. This throw would likely be made by an infielder or pitcher fielding a slow roller. The fielder's body is bent down to get the ball. When the ball is caught on the ground, the footwork is the same as for an overhand throw, but the throwing arm motion is straight back and the delivery and release are made underhand while the body remains bent over.

Both of these types of throws are much more difficult to control than the overhand throw. In certain situations, they can be an asset. It requires a lot of practice to develop consistent accuracy with sidearm and underhand throws. Work on developing them only after you can reliably make good overhand throws.

TAKE CARE OF YOUR ARM

A sore arm can wreck your season. Before you pick up a ball to throw, do a set of stretching exercises with your throwing arm. Try to feel your arm getting loose before starting to throw. When you start to play catch, start with short soft throws. Start to throw harder and at longer distances only after your arm feels warm and loose. If the weather is cool, you may start the warmup wearing a jacket. Discard the jacket when your arm feels loose, but put it back on when you are finished throwing to keep your arm from cooling down too quickly. Do not throw hard when the muscles in your arm feel tight or tired. Rest is the only real treatment for a sore arm; it can cost you playing time or severely limit your effectiveness if you continue to play.

THROWING PRACTICE

You have many opportunities to practice throwing when you are warming up before team practices or playing catch with a friend. Concentrate on developing good fundamental form when you're throwing. This includes all of the fundamentals outlined in this chapter, from the catch to the follow-through. You should practice these fundamentals until they become the natural way to make a throw. You know you have reached this point in your development when you can go through the throwing sequence without thinking about mechanics.

Start at a distance of about 30 feet from your partner. Try to make throws at your partner's chest. Experiment with different release points and with soft to hard throws. If your accuracy is good, move to a distance of 60 feet. This is the length of the base paths on the field. Again, make throws toward your partner's chest. It is important to *never* aim your throws. With practice, you should develop the skill to look at a target and come very close to it with a throw. To test your accuracy further, move back to 100 feet and play catch. To throw this far you will need to adjust both your release point and how hard you throw.

At about 60 feet, do a speed drill with your partner. This drill should help you develop a quick release. See how many accurate throws and catches you can make in a minute. Keep track of the number from session to session to gauge your improvement. Rushing throws can cause accuracy problems: Do not shortcut throwing fundamentals to gain a quicker release. To develop a quick release, stay with basic throwing fundamentals but go through all of the motions faster.

THINGS TO REMEMBER

1. Learn, practice, develop, and always use good throwing fundamentals.
2. Take care of your arm.
3. Develop a quick release.
4. Never aim your throws.
5. Experiment to find the most comfortable grip.

5

GET YOUR HEAD IN THE GAME

Up until this point, we have talked about the physical techniques of fielding and throwing. Before we go into specifics of position play, there is one more facet to cover. This element is the mental part of playing defense. We call this "having your head in the game," and it means that anytime you are in the field, you are totally aware of the game situation. You should know the score, the ball and strike count on the batter, the number of outs, and where there are runners on base. By glancing at the scoreboard you can get most of this information, but this is only a part of what you need to know to be a really good defensive player.

You must understand the game, anticipate, and know where to make plays based on the game situation. In the following chapters, we will cover most of the plays that should be made as we describe the responsibilities of each position. This can be the beginning of your study of the game. Your knowledge of the game will grow as you play and learn from your experiences and listen to your coaches. You will make mistakes as you play: Learn from your mistakes and from the things that go well.

BEING A VERSATILE PLAYER

Don't settle on playing only one position. Learn to play as many positions as possible. The fundamentals of fielding and throwing don't vary a great deal from one position to the next. If you have developed good solid basics, you can easily make the adjustments to move from one position to another. You are just starting a playing career. The more versatile you become, the more opportunities you will have to play as you grow and play at higher levels.

KNOW YOUR OPPONENTS

Having your head in the game goes beyond just knowing when to get a force out, double off a runner, or cover a base on a steal play. In league play, teams may play each other several times. Learning in games about other teams' strengths and weaknesses can give fielders on your team an edge. A fast runner on a team may steal a base the first time you play her team, but you'll be ready the next time she reaches base. A bunter may surprise the infield by dumping down a bunt and beating the throw to first for a base hit. She shouldn't surprise the infield again.

Outfielders may give a little extra room by playing a few steps back for the really good hitters on another team. But they should move in a few steps when the known weak hitters come to bat. Fielders should also look at a batter's timing relative to their pitcher's speed. A right-handed batter "pulls" the ball to left field, a lefty to right field. If the pitcher is really fast, few batters would be expected to pull the ball but they may pull a slower pitcher. Typically a right-handed batter facing a real fast pitcher, or a righty with a slow swing, will hit balls toward the "opposite" or right field. The opposite field hit from a left-handed batter goes toward left field. Adjustments fielders can make will be covered when we discuss specific position play.

STAYING FOCUSED

Having your head in the game and keeping it there is not always easy. There are many potential distractions during ball games that are created by fans or the other team. Or a pitcher may dominate batters so effectively that her defense sort of goes to sleep from lack of any action. Under any circumstances, good fielders have the discipline to block out all distractions and focus on their responsibilities as each pitch is delivered. If you can combine your knowledge of the game with your awareness of the game situation and focus on each pitch and anticipate plays, you are mentally prepared to be a good defensive player. You will have your head in the game.

6

PLAYING THE OUTFIELD POSITIONS

Now that you have a grasp of the fundamentals of all fielders, we will deal with the responsibilities of out-fielders in this chapter. The outfield is a relatively large space, making it necessary for the outfielders to act as a unit. All outfielders should be skilled in fielding and making throws. And we will put one misconception to rest right now. Some young players erroneously feel they are serving some type of sentence when they are assigned to play right field. Each position on the field is important and has certain responsibilities. There are cir-cumstances in games where the rightfielder may even get the most action.

THE CENTERFIELDER

The theory is that a strong defense is built "strong up the middle." This makeup includes the pitcher, catcher, shortstop, second baseman, and the centerfielder. The centerfielder should be the captain of the outfield. Players in this position are expected to take all fly balls they can reach, within reason, calling off other fielders with, "I've got it" or "Mine!" Because of the space to be covered, the centerfielder must have good foot speed and a strong arm.

THE LEFTFIELDER

Leftfielders make the shortest throws to the infield of all of the outfielders. There is not as much foot speed required for this position, compared to the centerfielder. Good right-handed hitters may pull long balls to left, especially if the pitcher throws at a slow or medium speed.

THE RIGHTFIELDER

Great foot speed isn't required to play right field. But the rightfielder makes the longest throws of all of the outfielders, making a strong arm an asset. There are plays where the rightfielder can play the part of an extra infielder and throw runners out at first or second.

And batters with slow swings will usually hit balls to right field.

OUTFIELD POSITIONING

The location where outfielders play hitters is a key to good defense. The coach may direct outfield positioning based on anticipation of where a batter may hit the ball. Positioning may be straightaway, back, in, left, or right. The objective of positioning is to help outfielders get to the ball as quickly as possible. As the outfield is being positioned, it is important for each player to move in coordination with the others. The outfield should move and change as a unit.

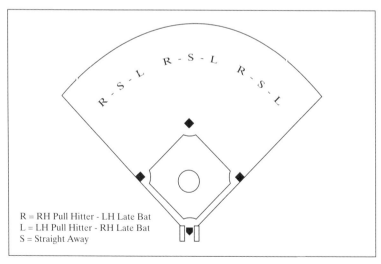

R = RH Pull Hitter - LH Late Bat
L = LH Pull Hitter - RH Late Bat
S = Straight Away

Outfield Shifts

Straightaway Position

The centerfielder is directly behind second base, in line with the base and home plate. The right and leftfielders are spaced an equal distance between the centerfielder and their respective foul lines. This can be thought of as the middle of a fielder's coverage area.

Shifting Left or Right

When the outfield shifts to one side or the other, players should keep the same distance between each other as in the straightaway position. The outfield may shift right or left when a pull hitter comes to bat. The shift would be toward the left field foul line for a right-handed pull hitter, toward the right field foul line for a left-hander.

When the shift occurs toward the left field foul line, the left- and centerfielders take five or six steps toward the line. The rightfielder shifts to the right the same distance and takes two or three steps in toward the infield. This is because the right-handed pull hitter's strength is to left field, and a ball hit to right field would not normally carry as far. If the shift is toward the right field foul line for a left-handed pull hitter, the leftfielder would move in a few steps.

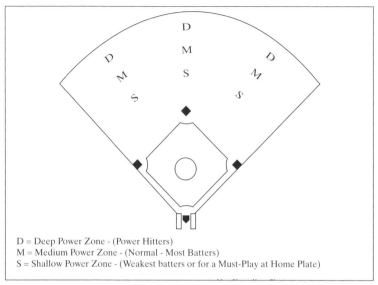

D = Deep Power Zone - (Power Hitters)
M = Medium Power Zone - (Normal - Most Batters)
S = Shallow Power Zone - (Weakest batters or for a Must-Play at Home Plate)

Outfield Depth

Playing Medium, Deep, or Shallow

When playing at medium depth, the outfielders should be positioned at about two-thirds of the distance toward the fence from the baselines. The outfield plays power hitters or long-ball hitters deep or back toward the fence, four or five steps from the middle position. A shallow position, when a weaker hitter is at bat, is four or five steps toward the infield from the middle position.

POSITION KEYS

First, if your coach tells you what position to take in the outfield, play where you're told. Good outfielders are

55

said to "get a jump on the ball." This means they can anticipate where a ball may be hit before the ball starts to travel. There are keys that can be used by outfielders to help in their position or in anticipating where balls will likely be hit.

The first set of keys can be gained by knowing a batter's position in the other team's batting order. In these examples, we will assume your team's pitcher has average speed. In a normal batting order, the first or leadoff batter and the second batter will be good contact hitters. Their goal is to reach base, and they may hit the ball anywhere in the field. You would normally play these batters straightaway and at medium depth. Many times these batters have good foot speed and may try to stretch a single into a double.

Batters three, four, and five will be the best hitters on the team. Normally, on medium-speed pitching they make good contact with power. You would shift a few steps toward their power field and back a few steps to a deeper position toward the fence. The opposite field outfielder would then move in three or four steps. Batters six through nine will be the weaker hitters on the team. The outfield would shift to a shallow position for these batters. And because weaker batters usually have a slower swing, you may shift a couple of steps away from their power field.

Pitch versus Bat Speed

A further set of position keys can be gained from watching a batter's bat speed in relation to your pitcher's speed. Remember: The power field for a right-handed batter is left field, and the opposite field is right; a lefty's power is to right field, the opposite field is left. If your team's pitcher is very fast, the better hitters on the other team may only be able to manage opposite field hits when they make contact. When this is the case, play the best batters in the early part of the lineup

Position to catch a fly ball

straightaway and all other batters to hit to the opposite field. In the lower half of the lineup, play right-handed batters as if they were left-handed pull hitters. If your pitcher's speed is unusually slow, you may play all batters in the top part of a lineup to pull the ball, and play the lower part of the lineup straightaway.

CALLING FOR FLY BALLS

When an outfielder calls for a fly ball, she believes she has it judged, can get to the ball, and can make the catch. To call for a fly ball, an outfielder yells in a loud voice, "I've got it," or "Mine!" Normally, the centerfielder will take any fly ball she can reach. But if the rightfielder or leftfielder calls for a ball, the centerfielder should pull up and let the other fielder make the catch. If both the centerfielder and another fielder call for the ball at the same time, the centerfielder should continue to call and make the play.

Short Fly Balls

On a short looping fly ball hit just over the infield, there is a chance that either an infielder or an outfielder can make the catch. There is the danger of a collision between the players. A rule to follow is that the outfielder moving in has an easier play than the infielder moving out under the ball. The outfielder should take charge and quickly call for the ball as soon as she sees she can make the play. The infielder should go after the ball until being called off by the outfielder, then pull up immediately.

BACKING UP OTHER OUTFIELDERS

When a ball is hit or thrown in your direction, you should move in to back up the play. The rightfielder backs up all ground balls hit toward first or second base and all throws to second base from the shortstop or third baseman. The centerfielder backs up all ground balls hit toward the middle of the infield and all throws toward second base from the vicinity of home plate by the catcher, pitcher, or first or third baseman. The left-fielder backs up all ground balls hit to the left side of the infield, all throws toward third base, and throws toward second base from the first or second baseman. The centerfielder should help right and leftfielders back up plays toward right and left center fields.

When a ball is hit toward the outfield, another outfielder should back up the outfielder making the play. When a ball is hit directly toward the centerfielder, both the right- and leftfielder move to back up the play. The centerfielder backs up all balls hit directly toward either the right- or leftfielder. If a ball is hit toward right center field and the centerfielder makes the play, the rightfielder is the backup. And if the rightfielder makes the play, the centerfielder is the backup. For balls hit toward left center, the left- and centerfielder have the same backup responsibilities.

THROWS FROM THE OUTFIELD

Base Hits

Unless an outfielder catches a fly ball for the third out to end an inning, she will need to make a throw somewhere. It is painful to watch an outfielder field a ball and then hold it, unsure of where to make a throw as runners circle the bases. Where to make a throw can be complex, but it is far better to throw to the wrong base than to hold the ball. This is a time when having your head in the game is very important. Each outfielder must think ahead about where to make a throw based on the game situation.

We will describe some typical plays in the following paragraphs. These are situations that apply when the ball is hit to medium depth and fielded cleanly. Generally, the throw should go ahead of the base the runner is advancing toward.

When there are no runners on base and a base hit goes to the outfield, the throw is normally to second base to hold the runner. But not all runners hustle to first base. And when the rightfielder is playing at a shallow or medium depth, she may be able to throw a batter-runner out at first base. To pull this play off, the ball must be hit hard and the rightfielder must make a quick, accurate throw.

When there is a runner on first, the throw after a base hit is normally toward third to hold the runner at second. But if the ball is hit hard and the runner going to second base loafs, either the rightfielder or centerfielder may double her off at second base. When throwing toward third, the infield cutoff player should be lined up between the outfielder and the base. The throw should be kept low so she can reach it if necessary. The infielder may cut the throw off if the runner holds or the throw is off direction or too short to reach the base.

With a runner on second, that runner may try to score on a base hit. On a play at home, the first baseman is usually the cutoff. She should be positioned near the pitcher's circle, ready to cut off the throw if necessary. The outfielder's throw should be toward home plate. This throw should also be kept low. When runners are on first and third, the runner on third will score on a base hit. The throw should go toward third to hold the runner at second.

Caught Fly Balls

These situations apply with less than two outs. When there are runners on base and the outfielder catches a fly ball or hard line drive, there may be an opportunity to double a runner off base. If the runner has left the base before the ball is caught, the infielders should tell the outfielder to throw to the base the runner left. Otherwise, the general rule after catching a fly ball with runners on base is the same as after base hits: throw to the base ahead of the runner. Runners may tag up and try to advance on fly balls when they are on second or third base.

Turn and run after a ball over your head.

Long Balls

A ball that is hit deep to the outfield presents a different challenge to outfielders. Balls hit over the outfielder's head or in one of the gaps between fielders must be chased down. In this case, the infield cutoff will move out into the field to cut off the throw and relay it toward a base. As soon as the outfielder gets the ball, she should make a throw to try to hit the cutoff at chest level. Other infielders will tell the cutoff where to make the relay throw. When a long fly ball is caught with runners on base, the throw again goes to the cutoff. She then will make a throw to get any runners who try to advance.

THINGS TO REMEMBER

1. Think ahead; keep your head in the game.
2. Remember your backup responsibilities.
3. A fielder moving in on a fly ball has the easier play.
4. Generally, throws go ahead of the runner.
5. Hustle to the ball.
6. Keep throws low; throw toward the cutoff's chest.

7

PLAYING FIRST BASE

With the exception of the pitcher and catcher, the first baseman is the busiest fielder. She will have batted balls hit her way and bunts dumped down her baseline. Over a season, she will lead the team in putouts as infielders throw runners out at first. She must be exceptionally good at fielding ground balls, pop-ups, and throws— some of which will be hard to handle.

CHARACTERISTICS OF A GOOD FIRST BASEMAN

A first baseman is usually taller than average, to make a large target for fielders when they make throws to first. All throws aren't always on target and may require the first baseman to do a lot of stretching and reaching to make the plays. A tall first baseman can reach throws that would be difficult for shorter players. A good first baseman has soft hands, good agility and footwork, and good body flexibility to make the stretches that may be required.

First base is the only infield position where a left-handed player has an advantage. A right-handed first baseman must turn her body to make throws to second or third base; a lefty doesn't need to do this. The lefty can cover more ground in the hole between first and second because her glove is on her right hand. A right-hander must make backhand plays in the hole. These are merely the advantages of a left-handed first base-man—but that does not mean a right-hander can't be-come very good playing this position.

POSITIONING

Unlike baseball, runners cannot lead off base. And be-cause a first baseman doesn't need to hold runners on base, positioning is somewhat simplified. The coach will signal when the first baseman should play in toward the batter. This will usually occur when there is an obvious sacrifice bunt situation or when the coach wants the in-field to make a play to home plate to prevent a run from scoring.

Normally, the first baseman sets up 10 or 12 feet from the first baseline and one step back of the base. Then there are adjustments to make, based on the batter. Left-handed pull or power hitters should be played two or three steps farther back and closer to the line. Right-handed pull hitters should be played two more steps to the right. Players who might try to bunt for a base hit should be played a couple of steps in front of the base. If your team has an exceptionally fast pitcher, play at the normal position when the top half of the order bats and move closer to the baseline for right-handed batters in the bottom half of the order. In the late innings, move two or three steps closer to the baseline than normal to guard against the possibility of an extra-base hit down the baseline.

MAKE THE CATCH

On all throws to first base, the first priority of the first baseman is to catch the ball, even if she must leave the base to make the catch. Infielders must field a ball and quickly make the throw to first to get the runner. Their throws aren't always accurate, and the first baseman must be prepared to deal with all kinds of throws. A ball that gets past the first baseman on a play at first usually advances a runner into scoring position at second or third base.

Receiving the Throw

As soon as a ball is hit in the infield, the first baseman should move to a position about 6 inches from the base, facing the fielder making the play on the ball. She should be in a solid balanced position, slightly bent at the waist and knees with her feet at shoulder width. Both hands should be chest high to make a target for the throw. As the ball is fielded, she should move her foot back to feel the base. A right-handed first baseman places her right foot on the base and strides with her

Target position for a good throw

left. The left-hander has her left foot on the base and strides with her right. As the fielder makes the throw, the first baseman strides toward the throw, keeping her foot in contact with the base as she makes the catch.

A Routine Play

When an infielder makes a clean fielding play and a strong accurate throw, the first baseman places her foot on the base, makes a short comfortable stride toward the throw, and catches the ball for the out. There are two things for the first baseman to remember. First, no matter how easy the play looks, she should never stride or get into a stretch position before the throw is on its way. Second, as soon as the catch is made, the first baseman should remove her foot from the base to avoid being stepped on.

Throws to the Side

The first baseman must be ready to stretch to reach throws to either side. On throws to the left, a right-handed first baseman makes a straight stride with the left leg. She must use a crossover stride with her left leg on throws to her left. The left-hander makes a straight stride with her right leg on throws to her right and a crossover stride on throws to her left.

Throw to the right

Throw to the left

High Throws

The first baseman should be prepared to jump to catch a high throw. The primary responsibility is to catch the ball; touching the base comes next. Ideally, the first baseman makes her jump so a foot lands on the base. This saves time spent trying to locate the base before the runner arrives.

Low Throws

A low throw that can be reached before it hits in the dirt by making a long stretch or a throw that hits in the dirt and takes a big hop are relatively easy plays at first base. The most difficult plays are on throws that hit the dirt close to the first baseman and must be "picked" or fielded on the short hop.

To pick a ball on the short hop, get the fingertips of the glove on the ground in front of the ball and scoop upward as it bounces. This is similar to catching a ground ball on a short hop. If the ball isn't scooped up cleanly, at least the ball is blocked and kept in front of the fielder. This is an impressive play when the ball is picked clean.

It takes a lot of practice to get good at scooping short hops. A good drill to practice scooping short hops requires another player. Back up near a fence where there is a good, clean, level dirt surface. Position a player at a distance of about 40 feet and have her throw balls in the dirt at your feet. Make the stretch and practice picking the throws. With practice, very few balls will get past you.

Wide Throws

When a throw is too wide to reach by stretching, the first baseman must leave the base to make the catch. If the throw is wide to the right, she must make the catch and try to step on the base before the runner arrives. If the throw is up the line toward home plate, the first baseman should catch the ball, grasp it firmly in both hands, and try to tag the runner before she reaches first base. The first baseman should be ready to apply a low tag in this case, because some runners try to slide into first when they see the throw up the line.

Throws from the Catcher

On a bunt or slow tapped ball along the first baseline, the throw from the catcher or pitcher fielding it will be close to the runner. On this play, the first baseman's receiving position changes. She should place her left foot on the base and take a sideways step toward second base, facing the fielder. This gives the fielder making the throw a large target to avoid hitting the runner.

When the catcher misses a pitch for a third strike and the runner runs toward first base, the throw from the

Target for throw from near the line in fair territory

Target for throw from foul territory

catcher will be in foul territory. The first baseman's receiving position for this throw is with the right foot on the base and the left foot in foul territory facing the catcher.

FIELDING PLAYS

Balls hit toward first base only add to the activity the first baseman gets. She must be skilled at fielding bunts, ground balls, line drives, pop-ups, and pop foul balls. Because most players bat right-handed and many balls hit toward first come spinning off of the end of the bat, the first baseman must often deal with crazy hops and pop-ups that curve in the air.

Unassisted Putout

Sometimes the first baseman fields a ground ball and can beat the runner to the base for an unassisted putout. When she tags the base she should step on the side of the base and get out of the runner's path. When a grounder is hit toward first, the pitcher should be moving to cover first base. When she can make the putout unassisted, the first baseman calls the pitcher off by yelling, "Mine," or "I've got it!"

Pitcher Covering First

When the first baseman must range far to the right or back to field the ball, the pitcher covers first base. As the ball is fielded, the pitcher runs to just inside of the first baseline and moves up inside the line toward the base. The first baseman tosses the ball to the pitcher as she nears the base. The pitcher completes the play by stepping on the inside of the base and turning left toward the infield to avoid the runner. How the first baseman tosses the ball depends on how far she is from the base. If she is close, a soft underhand toss should do. When the first baseman is farther away from the base, it may be necessary to make a soft overhand snap throw. This play takes good timing on the part of both the pitcher and first baseman. It should be practiced often as a part of team practice drills.

Fielding Bunts

Coaches set up all kinds of bunt defenses. Variations as far as the first baseman is concerned are either to charge or stay back. One option is where the pitcher covers all bunts toward first base. In this alignment, the first baseman plays at her normal position. If the first baseman is to charge in on bunts, she should move two or three steps toward home plate from the base and charge in when the batter squares.

When the first baseman fields a bunt, the catcher or another player will tell her where to make the throw. The second baseman will cover first. When the base call

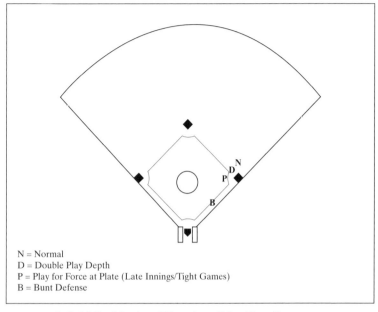

N = Normal
D = Double Play Depth
P = Play for Force at Plate (Late Innings/Tight Games)
B = Bunt Defense

Infield Positioning (Situational) for First Basemen

is made, the first baseman—without hesitating—must turn and square her body and make a quick, hard, accurate throw to the base that was called.

Pop-Ups

The first baseman goes after pop-ups behind first base in both fair and foul territory. She should go back hard to make a catch, unless she is called off by the rightfielder. The rightfielder will have an easier play moving in on the ball than any player moving toward the outfield. Following the same principle, the first baseman will have an easier play than either the pitcher or catcher and should take any pop-ups she can reach between first base and home plate.

Force Outs

It is always good to put out a lead runner whenever possible. Getting lead runners can kill rallies, prevent the other team from scoring, and result in winning games. But getting a lead runner on a ball hit to first base is not very easy. A fielder can't go too far wrong by getting an out, and that is always an option. However, with a runner on first base and less than two outs, the first baseman may be able to force the runner at second if she cleanly fields a hard-hit ground ball. If the ball is a slow roller, she should take the out at first. When the coach tells the infield to play in with the bases loaded and less than two outs, there is no decision to make. The play on any ground ball is to home to force a runner.

Cutoff Plays

A cutoff play involving the first baseman occurs when there will be a play on a runner at home plate. The first baseman is usually designated to be the cutoff in this situation. The cutoff moves to pitcher's-plate distance from home plate, directly in line with the fielder making the throw and the catcher. As the throw comes in, the catcher will instruct the cutoff how and where to make the play. If the catcher says "Let it go," or "No," the cutoff lets the ball pass to the catcher. If the catcher calls "Cut four," the cutoff catches the ball and makes a quick snap throw to home plate. Cut two or cut three means the cutoff catches and throws to the base called.

8

PLAYING SECOND BASE

The second baseman is another component of the defense that is strong up the middle. The second baseman's primary job is to field ground balls and throw out runners. Other than being the likely captain of the infield, the second baseman has responsibilities that are similar to the shortstop. And on many plays, the second baseman and the shortstop act as a coordinated team. Communication between these two infielders is important to properly execute plays, which keeps the defense strong.

CHARACTERISTICS OF A GOOD SECOND BASEMAN

The second baseman should have quick feet so she can cover her area to field ground balls, pop-ups, and line drives. Because the throws to first and second base are relatively short distances, she doesn't need a strong arm. To play the position well, the second baseman should have soft hands and a quick release. She must be a fundamentally sound fielder, make accurate throws, and have her head in the game at all times.

POSITIONING

The normal straightaway position for the second baseman is about two-thirds of the distance between first and second base, and four or five steps back of the baseline. The second baseman plays in this position for most batters when there are no runners on base. This deep position gives ample time to get to balls hit to either side and cut off base hits. There is also time to make the short throw to first base to get the batter-runners out. The second baseman should play at the normal position until there is a reason to adjust. There are two sources of information that can cause a second baseman to make a position adjustment to get a jump on where balls are likely to be hit. These shifts or adjustments are not big moves—just two or three steps.

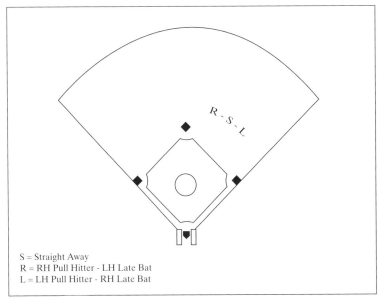

Infield Positioning for Second Basemen

First, the person keeping the score book should tell the defense where each batter hit the ball when she batted. If the scorer says a batter pulled the ball, the second baseman should shift toward the batter's strong side. This is toward second base for a right-handed pull hitter, toward first base for a lefty. When the scorer says the batter hit to the opposite field, shift toward the batter's weak side.

Second, the fielder can look for keys in the batter's timing relative to the pitcher's speed. If the pitcher is extremely fast, expect batters to have a late bat, especially in the lower half of the batting order. Play right-handed batters two or three steps closer to first base and left-handed batters two or three steps closer to second base. If the pitcher has average or slow pitch speed, play left-handed batters three steps closer to first base and right-handed batters three steps closer to second base.

Double Play Depth

With less than two outs, when there is a runner on first base, the second baseman moves to double play depth. This position is one step back of the baseline, keeping any adjustments made for the batter. This "in" position gives the shortstop/second baseman combination an opportunity to execute a double play by forcing the runner at second base and throwing out the runner at first base. It is difficult to make the double play at the youth level. However, a ground ball to either the shortstop or second baseman should result in forcing the lead runner at second base.

Playing In

With a runner on third and less than two outs in a close game, the coach may tell the infield to play in. This positioning is set up to try to prevent a run from scoring.

The second baseman moves to one step inside the baseline. If the bases are loaded, the automatic play is a throw to home plate to force the runner. If the bases are not loaded, the second baseman fields the ball and looks at the runner on third. If the runner breaks toward home, she should be thrown out. If the runner holds, the second baseman throws to first base for the out. This is called "looking the runner back."

FIELDING PLAYS

Most of the fielding plays the second baseman makes will be scooping up ground balls and throwing out runners. These plays are simple, but the second baseman has many other responsibilities. Several of these plays require communication and coordination with fielders at other positions. A good second baseman can execute all of the following plays well.

Pop-Ups and Fly Balls

When a second baseman can get to a pop-up or fly ball in her area, she calls a loud "I've got it," or "Mine," and makes the catch. The second baseman goes after fly balls and pop-ups in both fair and foul territory in short right field and on the right side of center field. Either the right- or centerfielder will have an easier play because she is moving in on balls in the short outfield. The second baseman should go hard after the ball but be ready to be called off if an outfielder can make the play.

Covering Bases

When there is a runner on first base, expect an attempted steal on each pitch. The second baseman and shortstop must talk and agree who will cover the base. As soon as the pitch passes the batter, move toward second base to get a head start on the runner. On a steal at second, it is normal for the second baseman to cover the base when there is a right-handed batter at the plate. The shortstop normally covers the base when there is a left-handed batter. The coverage may be changed if either the shortstop or second baseman has shifted position.

The second baseman covers first base on a bunt defense when the first baseman charges in, and when the first baseman goes after a fly pop-up. If the first baseman goes far to the right to get a ground ball, the second baseman moves to cover first base but yields to the pitcher if she gets there to cover the base. The second baseman covers second base on balls hit to left field and center field.

Cutoff and Relay Plays

The second baseman is the cutoff for deep fly balls and

extra-base hits to right and right center field. She goes to a distance of about 90 feet from the outfielder making the play and raises both arms to make a target for the throw. If the hit is a single and there are no runners on base, the second baseman takes a position between the fielder and second base. The shortstop will tell the second baseman whether to let the throw go through to the base, cut it off and hold it, or make a relay throw to the base. If the call is to cut and hold, the second baseman should run the ball back to the infield.

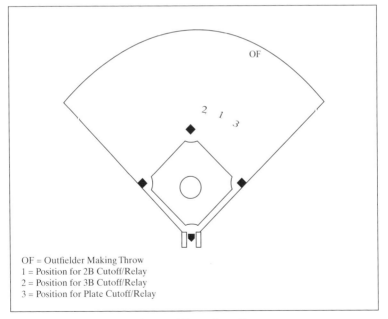

OF = Outfielder Making Throw
1 = Position for 2B Cutoff/Relay
2 = Position for 3B Cutoff/Relay
3 = Position for Plate Cutoff/Relay

Second Base Cutoffs

On an extra-base hit to the right side, or a caught fly ball with runners on base, the second baseman lines up to take the throw at a point halfway between home plate and third base. She receives the throw from the outfielder with her body turned slightly to help make a quick relay throw. The shortstop should make the call to hold or throw to a base.

Backing Up Plays

With no runners on base, the second baseman backs up the first baseman on all throws to that position. She also backs up at second base when the shortstop is covering the base. The second baseman backs up the pitcher on throws from the catcher.

Making Tags

When she is to cover second base, the second baseman should sprint to the base. Her feet should be straddling the base and facing the fielder making the throw. When the throw comes in, she must first concentrate on catching the ball, even if leaving the base is necessary. After the catch she should grasp the ball in her bare hand inside the glove and apply the tag to the runner. To make a good tag, the glove should be in front of the base, touching the ground. Keeping the glove low prevents the runner from sliding under the tag.

Always make tags low in front of the base.

Double Play

With less than two outs and a runner on first, or runners on first and second, the second baseman moves in to double play depth. She must first make sure to field a ground ball hit to her position. As she receives the ball, she pivots on her right foot and steps toward second base, tossing the ball to the shortstop for the force at second. The toss should be soft if the ball is fielded close to the base, and harder if the ball is caught farther away from the base. The shortstop will try to complete the double play by throwing the ball to first base.

When a ground ball is hit to the shortstop, the second baseman sprints to the bag, ready to catch the throw. If the throw is right on target, she receives it as she steps over the base with her right foot. She tags the base by dragging her left foot across it, then steps toward first to make the throw. On a throw to her left, she makes the catch, tags the base with her right foot, then steps toward first with the left foot to make the throw. She steps out with her right foot to make a catch on a throw to her right, drags her left foot across the base, and strides with her left foot toward first to make the throw.

When the second baseman fields the ball close to second base, she may call off the shortstop, tag the base,

Drag the foot across the base for force, then throw to first.

and make the throw. If it is a hard ground ball, this may be a sure double play. When she fields a ground ball near the baseline, the second baseman may be able to tag the runner advancing to second base. The ball should be held firmly in the glove with the bare hand when the tag is applied. If the ground ball is a slow roller, there may not be time to force the runner at second. In this case, the second baseman should throw to first for a sure out.

A second baseman and shortstop combination must practice a lot to get the timing and footwork right for turning double plays. The footwork is difficult for the second baseman because her momentum when she takes the throw is away from first base. She must catch the throw, tag the base, then turn and make an accurate throw. With practice, the routine can become automatic.

9

PLAYING SHORTSTOP

The shortstop is usually the best athlete on a team. This is a key position in a defense that is strong up the middle. She will play a leadership role in the infield by communicating with other infielders and coordinating plays with the second baseman. It is unusual to see a good defense that does not include a very good shortstop.

CHARACTERISTICS OF A GOOD SHORTSTOP

The shortstop must have quickness and speed to get to balls hit up the middle toward second base and to hits in the hole between her position and the third baseman. She must be a fundamentally sound fielder with soft, quick hands, a quick release when making throws, and a strong, accurate arm. She always has her head in the game. The shortstop or catcher may be the player who calls out to remind other fielders of the number of outs and where plays should be made.

POSITIONING

The normal straightaway position of the shortstop is about one-third of the way between second base and third base. There isn't a lot of time to make plays from shortstop to first base, and the throws are usually the

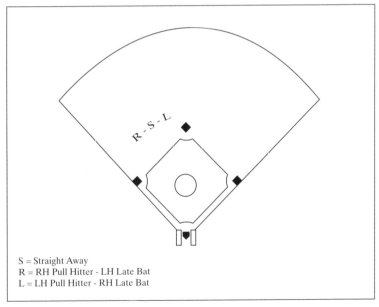

S = Straight Away
R = RH Pull Hitter - LH Late Bat
L = LH Pull Hitter - RH Late Bat

Infield Positioning for Shortstops

longest in the infield. She may play up to five steps back of the baseline if she has good range, a quick release, and a very strong arm. If her arm is average, she should gain time to make the plays by moving closer to the baseline.

Similar to other infielders, the shortstop will normally set up in the normal position. But she can adjust her position when she sees clues that help her anticipate where a batter may hit the ball. She can get information where a batter hit the ball the last time at bat from the scorer. Again, the shortstop should watch the pitcher's speed relative to a batter's timing. Few batters will pull hits off of a fast pitcher. The shortstop should play straightaway on batters in the top half of the batting order and shift to the weak side (toward second base for right-handed batters, toward third base for lefties) for batters in the lower part of the order. If the pitcher is average to slow, expect batters in the top of the order to pull the ball to their strong side and play straightaway on the lower half of the batting order.

Foul balls can help give clues. A batter that fouls off a pitch straight back to the backstop has the pitcher's speed timed. This batter will likely hit straightaway. A right-handed pull hitter may pull a foul ball down the third baseline. The shortstop should adjust into the hole toward third base. A late-swinging right-handed batter fouls balls toward the first baseline. This batter should be played toward second base. In the absence of good clues, the shortstop should keep in mind that the strong hitters occupy the top of the batting order. There are few candidates for the league batting title in the bottom half of a batting order.

Double Play Depth

With a runner on first base and less than two outs, the shortstop should move to double play depth. This position is a couple of steps back of the baseline. The shallower

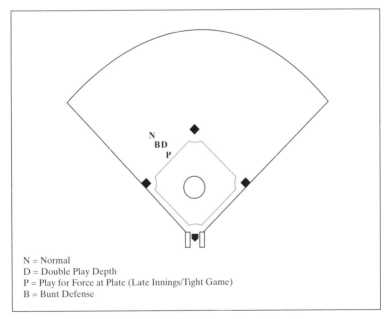

N = Normal
D = Double Play Depth
P = Play for Force at Plate (Late Innings/Tight Game)
B = Bunt Defense

Infield Positioning (Situational) for Shortstops

set-up gives the shortstop and second baseman an opportunity to try to make a double play. In the earliest years of league play, double plays are seldom executed. But the shortstop/second baseman combination should be able to force the lead runner at second base.

Playing In

In a close game with a runner on third base, the coach may pull the infield in to try to throw a runner out at home plate. When she plays in, the shortstop moves to the baseline. If the bases are loaded, the automatic play is to home plate to force the runner. If the runner at third is not forced to go, but tries to score, the shortstop should throw her out. If the shortstop looks the runner back to third base, she then throws out the runner at first base. A runner who strays too far off third base may be picked off with a quick throw.

FIELDING PLAYS

Most of the fielding plays made by a shortstop will be ground balls and throwing out runners at first base. But because of the ground to be covered by this position, the shortstop must also go after pop-ups, short fly balls, and catch line drives. Some of these plays will be a challenge to her speed and ability to judge fly balls because they require her to make over-the-shoulder catches.

Pop-Ups and Fly Balls

The shortstop goes after fly balls and pop-ups in short left and center fields and even foul balls behind third base. When she goes out to make these plays, she must be ready to be called off by an outfielder in position to make the catch. The shortstop calls a loud "I've got it," or "Mine," when she is in position to make a catch. Because she is moving in toward the ball and has the easier play, the shortstop should call off other infielders and make the catch when a pop-up is hit in the pitcher's area.

Covering Bases

When there is a runner on first base, an attempted steal is always possible. The shortstop or second baseman can cover second base on steals, but some teams designate that the shortstop always covers second. Normally, the shortstop covers second base when a left-handed batter is at the plate. The second baseman covers when the batter is right-handed. However, the two infielders must communicate and agree on who has coverage. When the second baseman covers the base, the shortstop backs up the play.

Cutoff and Relay Plays

When a ball is hit to left or center field, the shortstop goes out into the field to catch (cut off) a throw from an outfielder and make a relay throw. The shortstop should set up from 90 to 100 feet from the outfielder and in line with the base where a play is anticipated. She should hold up both arms to give the outfielder a good target for her throw. When a single is hit with the only runner on first base, the shortstop should line up between the outfielder and third base. If there is a runner on second and a single is hit, the shortstop lines up between the outfielder and home plate. Extra-base hits or balls that get past an outfielder usually require that the shortstop lines up with a point between second base

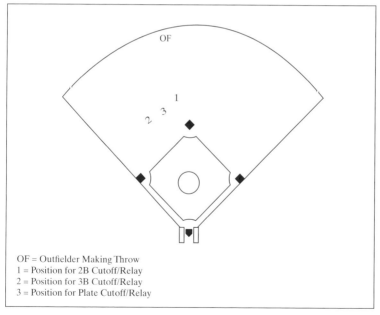

OF = Outfielder Making Throw
1 = Position for 2B Cutoff/Relay
2 = Position for 3B Cutoff/Relay
3 = Position for Plate Cutoff/Relay

Shortstop Cutoffs

and third base. The infielder covering the base on all cutoff plays should tell the shortstop to let the throw go through, cut it off and hold, or cut it off and throw to a base. If the call is to cut and hold, this means the runner or runners have held on base. The ball then should be quickly carried back to the infield.

Making a Tag

To make a tag on a runner, the shortstop sets up with her feet straddling the base, facing the player making the throw. She must first make sure to catch the ball. If it is a bad throw, she must leave the base to make the catch, then try to make the tag. When the tag is applied, the ball is held securely in the bare hand inside the glove. The glove should be held right on the ground in front of the base where the runner will slide into the tag. Holding the glove high may allow the runner to slide under the tag. One-hand tags and swipe tags are not good because the ball can easily become dislodged.

Double Play

With less than two outs and a runner on first, or with runners on first and second, the shortstop and second baseman move in to double play depth. When the shortstop fields a ground ball, the play is a toss to the second baseman covering second base. The toss should be at the second baseman's chest, making it easy for her to handle. The first objective is to get the force play on the lead runner at second base. If the second baseman's relay throw to first completes a double play, it's extra good.

When the ball is hit toward the second baseman in the situation above, the shortstop must sprint to second base, place his foot firmly on the base to get the force out, and throw to first base to complete the play. One of the surest second-to-first double plays occurs when there is a hard ground ball fielded close to second base by the shortstop. She makes the force unassisted by quickly stepping on the base, then throws the runner out at first base.

Other Plays

A line drive to the shortstop presents an opportunity to double off any runner who has left a base. The shortstop must focus first on making the catch, then throwing out the runner. With runners on first and second base, after fielding a ball the shortstop may be able to tag a runner advancing toward third. Again, there are runners on first and second. When a ground ball passes in front of the runner going toward third base, the shortstop should have time to throw to the third baseman to force the runner. To get this force, the ball must be fielded cleanly and the throw must be quick and on target. The other option is to take a force at second base. Either play takes a runner out of scoring position.

10

PLAYING THIRD BASE

Third base is called "the hot corner." Right-handed pull hitters rifle hard shots down the baseline, left-handed "slap" hitters try to punch balls past third base, and bunters dump balls down the baseline. When the infield is pulled in, the third baseman is almost as close to the batter as the pitcher. Plays at third base do not happen in slow motion. Third base is no place for a timid fielder.

CHARACTERISTICS OF A GOOD THIRD BASEMAN

The third baseman must be tough to dig in and field hard shots toward her position. She needs to have a quick release and a strong arm to make the long throws to first base to retire runners. Her hands must be fast to field the hard-hit balls down the baseline. The area the third baseman must cover isn't large. Speed is not a requirement, but she must have quick feet for three or four steps to field her position well. The third baseman can allow no distractions: She must be focused and on alert when each pitch is delivered.

POSITIONING

The normal position for the third baseman is even with the base and about two steps from the baseline. Most bunts for either a sacrifice or base hit will be placed down the third baseline. In most bunt defenses, the third baseman must charge in to field bunts down the line. The positioning when a sacrifice bunt is expected, or for a batter who often tries to bunt for a hit, is three steps in toward home plate. As soon as there are two strikes on the batter, the third baseman should move back to the normal straightaway position. (This is because a foul bunt attempt with two strikes is an automatic out.)

The number three through five or six batters in the other team's lineup will usually be the power hitters and the ones most likely to hit a shot toward third base. The right-handed batters should be played a step or two behind the base and two steps from the baseline. For the left-handed power hitters, the third baseman should stay back and move two more steps from the baseline.

If the pitcher has slow or average speed, the position is normal for batters other than the power part of the lineup. However, if the pitcher is fast, expect late-swinging batters in the lower part of the lineup. The position for the nonpower part of the lineup is three or four steps from the base for right-handed batters and two steps from the base for lefties.

In the late innings, the third baseman should play one step from the base to guard the line. The strategy is to prevent an extra-base hit down the baseline.

FIELDING PLAYS

Most of the fielding plays at third base are on ground balls and bunts. Many of these plays are routine when the ball isn't hit hard and is hit to the third baseman. She simply fields the ball and throws out the runner. But all plays at third are not routine. These are discussed below.

The Hard Shot

It is common for the third baseman to get two or three hard shots hit her way in each game. There is very little time to react, which is why quick hands and feet are necessary. There may only be time to make a quick stab with the glove to stop the ball. The third baseman must be alert and in the ready position on each pitch. If the hard-hit ball is fielded cleanly, there is ample time to make a good throw. Even if the ball isn't fielded cleanly but is blocked or knocked down, there still may be time to retrieve it and throw out the runner. If the hot shot is a line drive with runners on base, there may be an opportunity to double off a runner.

Slap Hitters

A slap hitter is always a left-handed batter. She will set up in the back of the batter's box. As the pitch arrives, she will take a running start toward first base and flick out the bat in an attempt to punch the ball into the infield and beat the throw to first base. A good slap hitter is also a very fast runner. The third baseman should suspect any left-handed batter in the top half of the batting order to be a slap hitter. Fortunately, most slap hitters give away their intention before they make contact with the ball. The third baseman's position doesn't change, but she needs to be extra-ready for some type of hit in her direction.

Bunts and Weak Ground Balls

Weak ground balls result when a batter doesn't make solid contact with the ball. These dribblers can make for tough plays because they are usually a surprise and require the third baseman to quickly move in a long distance to make the play. The obvious play on a dribbler is to take the runner going to first base. Quick hands and a strong throw are required to get the runner.

Bunts also require the third baseman to move in a long distance to make the play, but batters almost always square around before attempting to lay down a bunt. In most bunt defenses, the third baseman charges in. She breaks in toward the plate the instant she sees the batter square. If the bunt is rolling, it should be fielded in the glove using both hands. When a bunt has stopped rolling it should be picked up with the bare hand. When the third baseman is fielding bunts or dribblers, she takes most of them moving quickly toward home plate. A mistake many young players make is not getting their feet set and their body balanced before making the throw to first. It is better for the runner to beat out the play than to make a throw into right field, advancing the runner.

The third baseman should never try to umpire when a slow roller or bunt dribbles down the third baseline. If the ball is obviously going into foul territory, let it go. As soon as a ball rolls across the line into foul territory, swipe or hit with a glove, then it is automatically a foul ball. If the ball is near the baseline, she should make the

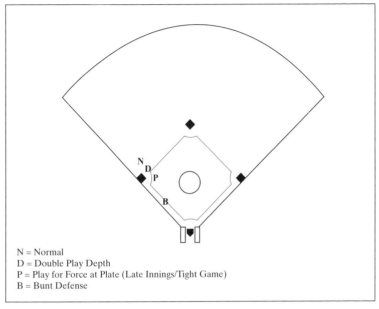

N = Normal
D = Double Play Depth
P = Play for Force at Plate (Late Innings/Tight Game)
B = Bunt Defense

Infield Positioning (Situational) for Third Basemen

play without hesitation and let the umpire make the fair or foul ball call.

Ground Balls to the Side

The third baseman doesn't have much ground to cover to her right. These are backhand plays on hard-hit balls, and she should be able to get in front of and block most balls near the base with a couple of sideways shuffle steps. The third baseman should take any ball hit to her left that she can reach. When the third baseman can cut off a ball in the hole toward the shortstop, it can accomplish one of several positive things. Getting to the ball in the hole may prevent a base hit. The play also negates the need for the shortstop to attempt a difficult backhand catch and throw to a base. The third baseman has more time to make the play because the throw is shorter and her momentum is almost toward first base. And, if there is a runner on first base, there may be an opportunity to get a force play on the runner at second base.

Force and Tag Plays

Any time there are runners on first and second and the third baseman fields a ground ball near the base, she may, if there is time, merely step on third base for a force out. She should make this play unassisted only when she is sure of beating the runner to the base. The other option is to throw out the runner at first. With less than two outs, a runner on second base who is not forced should be looked back to second base before the third baseman throws to first. If the runner breaks from second base, the third baseman should make a throw to pick her off.

The third baseman covers the base on all incoming runners. She must quickly get to the bag as the play develops. Her feet straddle the base, and she faces the player making the throw. Like other infielders, the first job is to catch the ball. She then applies the tag by holding the ball in her bare hand inside her glove. The glove is placed in low to the ground in front of the base to tag the runner.

Pop-Ups

The third baseman should handle all fair and foul pop-ups she can reach between third base and home plate. She will have an easier catch than either the pitcher or catcher, and should call for the ball as soon as she has it measured. The third baseman takes all pop-ups even with the base in either fair or foul territory. And she goes hard after pop-ups behind third base until she is called off by either the shortstop or the leftfielder.

11

CATCHER

Becoming a good catcher takes work and plenty of practice. The catcher carries a lot of responsibility for a team's defensive effectiveness. She is the only player who can see the entire field of play from her position, and her skills are vital to having a defense that is strong up the middle. She must be a smart student of the game to excel at the position. She gets action on each pitch in a game and must know how to react on every play. In many cases, the catcher will call the play to other team members.

And the catcher must be willing to get dirty. Foul tips can hurt, even through protecting equipment. Low pitches must be blocked and runners must be tagged out at the plate. Catching is hard work. It is not a job for the meek or faint of heart. However, good catchers wouldn't trade positions with any other player on the field. This position is only for those who really want to play behind the plate.

CHARACTERISTICS OF A GOOD CATCHER

Good catchers are aggressive, take-charge types. They play a leadership role on the team by calling plays and set a good example for teammates by hustling hard at all times. A good catcher is almost fearless. She accepts the risk of getting nicked by foul tips, but never blinks or flinches when a batter swings. The catcher must have a strong, durable body and good stamina. There is an average of about 17 pitches thrown per inning in a game. That computes to about 120 pitches in a regulation game. To give the signals to the pitcher and get into a receiving position will require that many deep squats in a game. Good catchers have staying power; they don't tire in the late innings.

A good catcher must have quick, soft hands to be a reliable receiver of pitches and throws. She will be required to catch or block most of those pitches mentioned in the preceding paragraph without having passed balls, even when the pitcher is wild. The catcher must also be able to field bunts and pop-ups. The good catcher also has a quick release and a strong accurate throwing arm. Runners will test a catcher and may steal everything but her equipment if she can't throw them out.

The catcher always has her head in the game; she must know the game to be able to call defensive plays to her teammates. She must also know how to work batters, to be good at giving signals to the pitcher and locations to hold the target for pitches. A good catcher knows the pitcher well and knows how to handle her. If the pitcher shows signs of stress, a good catcher would know when to call time out and go out to help her pitcher calm down; if the pitcher starts having control problems, the catcher may be able to give suggestions that help the pitcher get back on track.

Finally, a good catcher must have excellent self-control. She will not become flustered or distracted no matter how tense the game situation becomes. Remaining calm amidst the chaos of screaming players and fans is not easy. The good catcher keeps her cool and does her job.

THE CATCHER'S EQUIPMENT

The mask, shin guards, and chest protector are pieces of gear designed to protect the catcher from foul tips or bad pitches. Before getting behind the plate, the catcher must adjust each piece of equipment so it fits. There are two key areas where the equipment must be safe.

First, the mask and helmet must fully protect the face and head, and there should be a throat protector on the mask. The chest protector must also be adjusted high to cover the lower part of the throat. The shin guards should cover the instep on each foot. Although the equipment doesn't cover the catcher's entire body, these two vulnerable areas can be protected by well-fitting equipment.

At first, the catcher's equipment can feel awkward. To get conditioned to wearing it, the catcher should wear full gear when warming up pitchers, taking infield drills, or just playing catch. Eventually, if the gear fits, it will begin to feel as comfortable as the uniform.

The catcher's mitt should fit the hand and be broken in so the fingers "hinge" toward the thumb and palm of the glove when the ball is caught in the pocket or web. New gloves are stiff, and it is hard to keep a ball from popping out of the pocket. Glove oil can be used to soften the leather. Binding a ball in the pocket overnight with a rope or rubber binders can help loosen and form the mitt. However, nothing breaks in a new glove better than catching a lot of pitches.

THE CATCHER'S RESPONSIBILITIES

The catcher has many varied defensive responsibilities. She is involved in each play of a game and, in many cases, has several jobs on some plays. She starts each play by giving a signal to the pitcher. This is only the start of a play. In the following sections, we will examine the jobs of the busiest player on the defense.

Giving the Signal

The catcher gives a signal to the pitcher to suggest a pitch. The pitcher can shake off the signal if she wants to throw a different pitch. The pitcher's selection of a pitch will almost always be honored. It is important for both players to know and agree on which pitch will be used. In the earliest years of league play, the pitch selection will usually consist of only a fast ball and change-up. It is good for a young catcher to get into the habit of signaling pitches at the beginning of her career. Pitchers soon develop curves and sliders that are not only hard for batters to hit, but are also hard for catchers to receive if they don't know what is coming.

To give the signal, the catcher squats down in position behind home plate, making sure to be out of reach of the batter's swing. The body should be bent at the knees and waist; the back is straight. The feet should be about 10 inches apart with the toes and knees angled slightly outward. The left forearm should rest on the left knee with the glove placed with the palm inward to block the signal from being seen by the third base coach. The signal is given with the fingers of the bare hand held high near the right thigh and next to the catcher's crotch.

Signals are made up between the pitcher and catcher, but the simplest version is one for a fast ball, two for a change-up, a fist for a pitch-out, and three or four for any others in the pitcher's assortment. (It is common for the coach to call all pitch-outs when a steal attempt is anticipated.) The catcher may also signal for an inside or

Give the signal.

outside pitch by moving her hand to the inside of the thigh where she wants the pitch to be located. Coaches cannot steal a good catcher's signals. When there is a runner on second, the pitcher may have an alternate set of signals to prevent the runner from stealing them. One way is for the catcher to give two or three signals with only one being the real signal.

Giving a Target and Receiving

After giving the signal, the catcher goes into a receiving position. With the feet spread about shoulder width, the catcher's lead foot should be slightly ahead of the plant foot. The weight should be on the toes as the catcher bends the knees to go down to give a low target. The catcher should be balanced and set up just out of the batter's swing arc. In this position the catcher is ready to make the shuffle step to throw, sprint out to field a bunt, chase a pop-up, or drop down to block a low pitch.

With the arms bent at a 90-degree angle, the glove is held open, with fingers up and forward toward the pitcher. In most cases, the target should be low in the strike zone at about the height of the batter's knees. Depending on the pitcher's control, the target may be over a corner or down the middle of the plate. However, pitches down in the strike zone are the most difficult for batters to hit solidly.

Show the target.

The glove should be held still until the pitcher releases the ball. A catcher must focus on the ball, watching it all the way to the glove. Pitches above the waist should be caught with the fingers up, those below the waist caught with the fingers down. When a catcher has soft hands, the glove gives slightly as the ball is caught. The bare hand should cover and grasp the ball as soon as it hits the mitt to prepare for making a throw.

A catcher's fingers on the throwing hand are often injured by foul tips or reaching for the ball before it hits the mitt. The best way to prevent a finger injury is to make a fist with the bare hand with the thumb tucked

Protect the throwing hand by: making a tight fist, or

Holding the hand behind the glove

in the palm of the hand. Any ball that hits the knuckles will do far less damage than one that hits an open finger. Another method is holding the throwing hand behind the glove until the ball enters the pocket. Using either method, catchers must practice quickly covering and grasping the ball and getting set to throw.

Blocking Low Pitches

To block low pitches, the catcher must keep her body square in the path of the pitch and drop to both knees. The glove should be on the ground to scoop up the ball if possible. Many low pitches can be smothered by the

Drop down to block low pitches.

glove. Pitches that bounce in front of the plate will usually bounce high and must be blocked by the body. If a pitch can't be handled cleanly, the catcher must try to block the ball and keep it in front of her so she can quickly retrieve it and make a play.

Making Throws

Catchers who throw out runners attempting to steal bases make a big contribution to a team's defense. Potential base thieves exist on all teams, and they will test a catcher. After a catcher cuts down a few runners, coaches are hesitant to try to steal. A catcher who can't make the throws may give any runner a free pass into scoring position a couple of pitches after she reaches base.

A catcher should have a strong, accurate arm and a quick release. The need for arm strength and accuracy are obvious, but the ability to get off a throw quickly once the ball is received can be overlooked. Catchers who can't get off a throw quickly make late throws to the bases, even if the arm is strong. A quick release can make up for some lack of arm strength. Footwork must be efficient to develop a quick release. It starts with the receiving position where the feet are set to make the shuffle step and throw. The hands must also be fast to receive the ball, grip it, and cock the arm to throw. A good practice drill should be done wearing full catcher's equipment. Starting in the receiving position, the catcher takes throws from a pitcher and practices making throws to the bases. The footwork, hands, and arm action when throwing to bases should be quick and automatic.

The strongest throwing motion is straight overhand or three-quarter overhand. A young catcher should practice both actions to see which motion is most accurate. As a throw is received and the ball is picked out of the mitt, the arm movement is up and back to a cocked position. Young catchers may need to reach back to throw harder. But with growth and improved arm strength, the catcher can take the hand to a position just behind the ear and make a quick snap throw. A hard, accurate snap throw is a big part of having a quick release. Catchers who wind up to throw give runners a big advantage.

Footwork forms the foundation for good balance when making throws. As mentioned before, in the receiving position, the feet are set with the (left) lead foot slightly ahead of the (right) plant foot. As the ball is received, the catcher takes a small shuffle step with the plant foot, strides toward the target with the lead foot, and makes the throw. Some young catchers make the mistake of taking several steps before throwing, and their throws are almost always late. Receiving the ball, striding, and making the throw should be smooth and quick.

Receive the pitch and shuffle step.

Stride and reach back to throw.

Release the overhand throw.

Follow through.

Steal Plays

When there is a runner on first base and she tries to steal second base, throw her out. The catcher can see the runner going, but it is helpful if the first baseman yells "Steal," or "She's going!" when the runner starts to steal. When there are runners on both first and second, and there is an attempted double steal, throw out the runner at third. With runners on first and third there are several options, and coaches usually set up the defense.

When there are two outs and the runner on first tries to steal, a confident catcher may throw her out to end the inning. But some coaches won't risk giving up a run to try to get the out. Another play has the catcher throwing to third base, to pick off the runner there. Some teams throw to the pitcher, who tries to pick the runner off of third base.

The best play in this situation is like a sucker play on the runner at third. This play must be practiced a lot because it takes good timing and coordination. When the runner breaks toward second, the catcher makes a throw toward second base but it is low and short of the base. The shortstop cuts in front of second base, takes the throw, and cuts down the runner trying to score. This play can often work against a team with aggressive baserunners. It is a real rally killer.

Fielding Pop-Ups

When a pop-up leaves the bat, the catcher should immediately remove her mask. She should hold the mask until she finds the ball in the air, then throw the mask away from the area where the ball will come down. Foul pop-ups behind the plate are the catcher's responsibility. They should be caught with both hands, palms up, near the chest.

Any fielder moving in to catch a pop-up has an easier play than the catcher going out under the ball. The first or third baseman should call for and take any pop-ups between her position and home plate. The catcher, however, should move out under these pop-ups and try to make the catch until she is called off by another fielder.

Short pop-ups are usually easy to judge and catch because they go up and come straight down toward the ground. Real high pop-ups react differently in the air due to the spin caused when the ball contacted the bat. The spin causes the ball to come down with what is called "infield drift." In effect, the ball ascends to the apex of flight, and the spin causes it to curve toward the infield as it comes down. To play a high pop-up, the catcher should circle beyond the spot where the pop-up will come down and turn her back toward the infield. In this position, the ball will descend toward her.

Fielding Bunts

In a receiving position, the catcher's feet are placed to initiate a throw. And the foot placement is also almost in a sprinter's ready position. This helps the catcher quickly sprint out to field bunts in front of the plate. When a bunt goes down, the catcher flips the mask and helmet off the back of her head and goes after the ball. Generally, bunts that travel no more than three or four steps from the plate are the catcher's play. When the catcher is going to make the play, she must call off other fielders, saying "I've got it" as she approaches the ball.

The catcher circles to the left of bunts when she makes the play. The circle must be wide when the bunt is down the third baseline, and the throw must go to first base. The circle is less when the bunt is toward the pitcher, and even less when the bunt goes down the first baseline. If a catcher's footwork is correct, a line across the toes as the ball is fielded will point toward the base where she is making the throw.

A bunt that has stopped rolling should be scooped up with the bare hand. The catcher takes the shuffle step then strides and throws out the runner. When a bunt is rolling, the catcher should block it with her mitt and scoop it into her throwing hand in one motion. Then she sets her feet to make the throw.

Bare hand pickup

Scoop up a rolling bunt.

Bunts out of the catcher's range will be played by the third baseman, pitcher, or first baseman. Because the catcher can see the field, and the fielder is facing away from any play, the catcher should call out the number of the base to make the throw. In any case, when the ball is bunted there is a play at first. However, with runners on base, a force play may be possible when the ball is bunted hard toward a fielder. It is a judgment call by the catcher to call for the other fielder to force a lead runner at second or third base. Again, getting out lead runners can kill rallies.

Covering Home Plate

Any time there is a play at the plate, the chips are down. It is the catcher's job to cover the plate, make a tag, and prevent a run from scoring. Unfortunately, all throws to the plate won't be on target. The first thing a catcher must do is catch the ball, even if she needs to leave the plate to handle a wide throw. If a throw is on target but is low, it should be blocked and scooped if possible. A catcher should never back up to play a throw on the bounce.

Making Tags

It is a rule that the catcher can't block the plate. A runner must have a path to the plate or it will be ruled as obstruction. To make the tag on a runner, the catcher

Low tag in front of the plate

places her left foot on the third base side of the plate and drops to the right knee on the back side of the plate. The ball must be held tightly in the bare hand inside of the pocket of the glove, and the glove should be held on the edge of the plate facing third base. This will give a runner a small access to the plate, but she should slide into the tag.

Force Plays

When the bases are loaded, there is a force play at home. The catcher should stand behind the plate, facing the player making the throw. If the throw is on target,

Target for force play at the plate

the catcher steps on the plate with her right foot and stretches forward to receive the throw with her left foot. If a throw is to the side, she should step out to receive the throw and drag the opposite foot across the plate to complete the play. With less than two outs, after getting the force at home, the catcher should be ready to throw to a base. She may be able to complete a double play by forcing the runner at first base.

Pickoff Plays

The runners can't lead off bases; they must wait until the pitcher releases the pitch. It is not productive for a catcher to bluff pickoff throws. The catcher and infielders should have a pickoff signal when a runner repeatedly wanders off base. A pitchout isn't necessary. After giving the signal, the catcher makes the pickoff throw after receiving the next pitch. The throw should be low on the infield side of the base so the fielder can easily make the tag.

Some runners will bluff a steal to try to draw a throw. If the runner isn't far off base, she may be picked off. However, some runners go halfway to the next base and stop. This is an attempted cute sucker play. If the catcher throws behind the runner, she will likely advance. Throwing ahead of the runner will prevent an advance. But when a runner has stopped between bases, she is a "sitting duck" and should be put out. The catcher should hold the ball behind her ear, ready to throw, and run straight at the baserunner. This makes the runner commit to a base where the catcher can throw her out or catch her in a rundown.

Working with the Pitcher

The pitcher and catcher make up the core of a team's defense. It is a partnership. How well they work together will determine, in large part, a team's success. The catcher must get to know the pitcher well from experience in practices, control drills, and games. The catcher should know how well the pitcher can control her pitches and if she can spot them in the strike zone. She should also know to call pitches the pitcher throws best, and what situations cause her the most trouble. She must know how to boost the pitcher's confidence and when to pick her up by giving encouragement when she gets down. She also needs to know how to help the pitcher deal with pressure situations. Knowing all these things and adjusting when necessary are what are referred to as "handling the pitcher." The best catcher knows her pitcher well and can help her be more effective in getting batters out. The catcher should be the pitcher's strongest supporter.

Working Batters

Fooling batters and getting them out is the most fun a pitcher and catcher can have in a ball game. Thinking and working together as a team pays big dividends. The catcher can see things that can make batters vulnerable and call for pitches that help get them out. The catcher should have a purpose for each pitch as she gives the signal and sets up the target.

It is always important for both the pitcher and catcher to know where they are in the other team's batting order, as well as the game situation. It is helpful to check with the team's scorer to see what each batter did the last time up. Working batters in the upper half of the other team's batting order will be different than how the lower half will be pitched.

The catcher should always try to help the pitcher get ahead in the count to each batter by throwing strikes and, when the pitcher is behind in the ball and strike count, call for pitches and hold the target to just throw strikes. The best pitch will always be a strike and it is even better if it is a low strike.

There are some keys to a batter's weaknesses that the catcher can see as the batter sets up; other keys can be observed after one or two pitches.

Late bat This late swinger will usually be in the low part of the batting order. When she swings at a pitch, the ball is in the catcher's mitt before the bat goes through the strike zone. A change-up or off-speed pitch should never be thrown to a batter with a late swing. It is the only type of pitch she can hit. This batter should get a steady diet of fast balls.

Scared batter Some batters set up so far from the plate that they can't reach a pitch down the middle. This batter can be struck out with pitches on the outside half of the plate.

Plate crowder This batter sets up almost "hanging ten" over the inside part of the plate. This tactic is taught by some coaches. The batter is attempting to take the plate away from the pitcher, drawing a base on balls. The catcher should call for inside pitches to the plate crowder. Pitches on the inside will result in only weak hits on the bat handle.

Beggar Some batters will not swing at even a perfect pitch. Batters like this are begging for a walk. This one will also be in the bottom of a batting order. Three pitches over the plate will send the beggar back to the dugout.

Pull hitter A pull hitter will stride down the baseline when she swings. This batter is attempting to hit with power. She wants a pitch on the inside part of the plate where she may be able to hit a long ball. Pitches on the outside part of the plate are almost impossible to pull, even by a strong pull hitter. They usually result in a weak infield ground ball.

Anxious batter This batter dances around in the batter's box like she has ants in her pants. She may take a lot of quick half-swings, wasting energy and building up stress. This could be a good hitter. The catcher can allow her to build up stress and get tight muscles by delaying the signal. This batter may also be gotten out with off-speed pitches.

Good hitter This batter has a straightaway stance. She will be in the top half of the batting order. She may foul a good fast ball straight back toward the backstop. This batter has the pitcher timed. She should be pitched carefully with low fast balls and speed changes to keep her off balance.

OTHER CATCHER JOBS

The catcher must hustle after any passed balls or wild pitches and make throws where appropriate. When there are no runners on base, the catcher backs up throws from infielders to first base. And with no runners on base, the catcher covers first when the first baseman goes after a pop-up or fly ball.

FINALLY

Other than the pitcher, the catcher is the busiest player on defense. Catching has many responsibilities, some bumps and bruises, and it is hard work. It is a position for only those players who really want to get behind the plate.

12

DEFENSE FOR PITCHERS

The moment the pitcher releases a pitch, she becomes another infielder. Her follow-through after each pitch should put her in a ready position similar to other fielders. The pitcher's primary responsibility is to throw strikes, but she has many more responsibilities as a fielder. The pitcher will have opportunities in each game to get batters or runners out with her fielding. Pitchers who allow runners to reach base safely or advance by poor fielding only make trouble for themselves and their team.

CHARACTERISTICS OF A GOOD FIELDING PITCHER

To field her position well, a pitcher must have quick hands and feet. In her follow-through and ready position, she is less than 40 feet from the batter. Many of the balls the pitcher must field are hard shots back through the box. You could class some of the catches she makes as acts of self-defense. The pitcher must have quick feet to get to bunts and cover or back up bases. Her throwing arm doesn't need to be particularly strong, but she should have a quick release with good accuracy to throw out runners at the bases.

FIELDING PLAYS

The pitcher should be included in all team infield practices and pregame warm-ups. Teams that overlook this aspect of defense training will lack the coordination and timing that is vital to a good defense. The pitcher above all other fielders should have her head in the game. This means that before each pitch she has evaluated the game situation and knows where to make a play when she fields a ball.

Comeback Hits

Good pitchers seem to get a lot of balls hit back to them. These are easy plays when there are no runners on base. She fields the ball, steps toward first base, and throws out the runner. If it is a hard comeback hit, there is ample time to make the play. With a softer comeback, there is less time, but this play is still not difficult.

With runners on base, a hard comeback hit with less than two outs presents an opportunity to prevent runs and kill the other team's rally. The pitcher is in the middle of the infield, close to all of the bases. The runners can't lead off of the bases. Unless a runner is attempting to steal a base with the pitch, the pitcher will have time for a force play. When there is only a runner at first base, there is a force at second. And with runners on both first and second, she should force the runner going toward third base. With the bases loaded, the play is a force at home plate. If the pitcher bobbles the ball, there should still be time to throw out the batter-runner going to first base.

When there are runners on second or third but no runner on first, there isn't a force play. When the ball is fielded, the pitcher should look the runner or runners back to the base and then make the play at first base, if the runners hold. If a runner breaks toward a base, she should be thrown out. When a runner starts to advance and then stops between bases, the pitcher should run straight at her. The pitcher then should throw the runner out if she tries to advance, or trap her in a rundown.

Line drives or soft looping fly balls hit to the pitcher may present an opportunity to double off any runner who had left the base when the ball was contacted.

Slow Ground Balls

The pitcher knows where plays should be made, but there may not be time for any play other than to first base when she fields a slow roller. Because she can see the whole field, the catcher is in the best position to call the base where the play should be made when there are runners on base. If there is time to force a runner, the catcher should call the base by yelling, "Go two," or "Go three!" Getting an out is always good, and there is usually the out at first.

Fielding Bunts

A pitcher must be good at fielding bunts and throwing out runners. Bunt defenses set up by coaches vary, but in any set-up, the pitcher is expected to handle bunts in some part of her area. Smart teams will test a pitcher's ability to make the plays when the ball is bunted. And they may dump bunt after bunt until the pitcher proves she can get the runners out. A pitcher who can't reliably handle bunts can literally be bunted out of a ball game. A smart pitcher will spend a lot of practice time fielding bunts and making the throws.

When a bunt is rolling, the pitcher should block it with the glove and scoop it into her bare hand. She then grips it, sets her feet, and makes the throw. She picks up bunts that have stopped rolling in her bare hand and makes the throw. Bunts that are obviously rolling across the foul line should be allowed to roll into foul territory, then touched with the glove or bare hand.

If a bunt is popped up, there may be an opportunity to double off a runner. And hard-hit bunts may allow a force play when there are runners on base. This is another situation when the catcher should make the call.

A bunt defense includes the possibility of coverage by the catcher, pitcher, first baseman, and third baseman. The player fielding the bunt should quickly call off all other fielders as she moves in to make the play.

Making the Throws

Some throws the pitcher makes are simple. Hard comebacks and throws to first base or home plate are merely a matter of stride and throw, using good fundamentals. On other plays, the pitcher's momentum may be away from the target, or it may be necessary to turn the body to make the throw. This is where practice helps. Many young pitchers try to hurry a throw without first being balanced with the feet set. It is much better to make a good throw that arrives late than to make a throw the other fielder can't handle.

Covering Bases

When a ground ball goes to the first base side of the infield, the pitcher goes toward first base to cover. If the first baseman fields the ball and calls off the pitcher, she will make the play unassisted. When the first baseman leaves the base to field the ball and either she or the second baseman fields it, the pitcher must continue toward first base to take a throw. When moving to cover first base, the pitcher should sprint toward a point on the foul line about 10 feet from first base, then turn and run inside the baseline toward the base. This direction avoids a collision with the runner. The pitcher takes the throw from the other fielder and tags the inside of the base with her right foot to get the out. After tagging the base, the pitcher should turn to the left to stay out of the runner's path. The pitcher must hustle to make the play. This play should also be practiced extensively to get the timing right between the pitcher and fielders.

When the shortstop and second baseman go into the outfield after a fly ball, the pitcher covers second base. If the shortstop and third baseman go into left field after a fly ball, the pitcher covers third base. The pitcher covers home plate when there is a runner in scoring position

Pitcher covers first

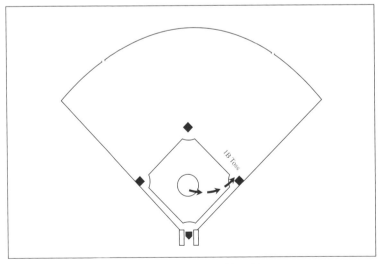

Pitcher Path Covering First Base

and the catcher goes after a pop-up, or after a pitch that gets past the catcher. To make a tag, the pitcher must sprint to the base and straddle it, facing the player making the throw. She must catch the throw and hold the ball securely in her bare hand inside the glove. The glove should be placed low in front of the base. In no case should the pitcher attempt to block the base.

Backing Up Bases

When there are runners on base or when there is an extra-base hit, it is the pitcher's responsibility to back up plays at third base and home plate. She must anticipate where the play will be and take a position about 20 feet behind the base in line with the incoming throw. This distance should provide enough time to back up the play if the ball gets past the player covering the base.

Generally if there is a runner at first base and the batter gets a single, the pitcher backs up third base. When there is a runner on second base and the batter gets a hit, the pitcher backs up home plate. If the batter hits a fly ball to the outfield with a runner on third base, the pitcher backs up home plate. It can be difficult to tell which base to back up when there is an extra-base hit. The pitcher should go to a point about halfway between home plate and third base and move to the proper backup position as the play develops.

13

PROFILE OF A GAME-WINNING DEFENSE

Successful teams play good defense. Defensive strength keeps the team in each ball game by making it difficult for the other team to score. Teams put pressure on a defense by aggressive hitting, bunting, and aggressive base running. Close games are normal in fast pitch softball. In our experience, there are more games that are lost by defenses that can't stand up to the pressure and make the plays than games that are won with an overpowering offense. The winning defense described in this chapter doesn't crack under pressure.

FUNDAMENTALS

A winning defense is fundamentally sound at all positions. Fielders are aggressive yet controlled as they make the proper plays. They field throws, ground balls, and fly balls with sure, soft hands. Their footwork is solid, and their throws are crisp and accurate. The mechanics of covering bunts, turning double plays, executing cutoff and relay plays, and backing each other up show the team operating as a coordinated unit. Much of this depends on how well a coach has prepared the defense, and individual players must practice hard to gain a high level of skill.

STRONG UP THE MIDDLE

The construction of a good defense is "strong up the middle." Positions making up this alignment are the catcher, pitcher, shortstop, second baseman, and centerfielder. Players at all of these positions must be very adept at handling their responsibilities. The theory is that most of the plays in a game will be handled by these positions, but this is not to minimize the need for skill at all other defensive positions. For example, if a pitcher is fast, the rightfielder may get most of the fly balls in a game hit toward her position. Or a team that bunts frequently may require the third baseman to make a lot of plays. All positions are important and each player has responsibilities to handle.

READY

All players are loose and ready to make a play when each pitch is delivered to the plate. Each fielder's body is in the ready position, focused on the pitch. As the pitch reaches the batter, fielders' feet are moving slightly with little shuffle steps. This shows that each fielder is on her toes, ready to get a quick start toward any batted ball.

HEADS IN THE GAME

Each player has her head in the game. She knows the game situation and listens to the coaches and captains as they call out reminders of where plays should be made. Players know when to anticipate bunt and steal attempts, and where to make force plays. Each player knows her responsibilities: when to cover a base, act as the cutoff, or back up a play. Players communicate where to make a throw and call for fly balls and pop-ups when they will make the catch. Other teammates respect the calls and pull up when they are called off the play.

A winning defense knows that getting lead runners out can prevent the other team from scoring. Whenever possible, they take force-outs at second or third base to keep runners farther away from scoring position. When there are runners on base who are not forced, they know how to look them back to a base before taking an out at first base. A winning defense makes very few concessions. With less than two outs and runners on first and third, there will be a play if the runner on first tries to steal. The play may be an attempt to pick the runner off of third base, or a cutoff to get the runner trying to score. Only a weak defense or a team with a big lead will concede a steal, placing a runner in scoring position at second base. And when playing with a big lead in the late innings, a team may allow a runner at third to score on a ground ball to the infield, trading a run for an out at first base.

When a runner is trapped off of a base, the fielders know they must chase the runner back toward the preceding base. If the runner isn't caught and tagged or thrown out, she won't advance. From practicing rundowns, they know the less throws made in a rundown the better.

CONFIDENCE AND TRUST

Players on a winning defense have confidence in their own abilities, and also in the abilities of their teammates. These players work together as a unit, communicating with each other and handling the responsibilities of their positions. They trust each other. It starts with a pitcher who feels she can throw any pitch without the catcher having passed balls, or with the pitcher who throws strikes, trusting that her defense will make the plays.

A winning defense doesn't just happen. It is the result of a coach's emphasis and frequent practice. It requires players to develop and constantly improve their individual skills. And finally, it requires each player to study, learn, understand the game, and keep her head in the game.

14

COMMON FIELDER PROBLEMS

In this chapter we will summarize common problems in fielding fundamentals that plague young players. These lapses in concentration or technique can result in errors that cause a team to lose games. There is no excuse for a player who does not have her head in the game or does not know where to make a play when the opportunity arrives, or one who is not in the ready position on each pitch.

HANDLING THE GLOVE

Attempting one-handed catches Young players should try to make one-handed catches only when it is the only way to reach the ball. Two-handed catches are the surest way to make plays.

Fingers up, fingers down Balls will be missed frequently when a fielder tries to catch balls below the waist with the fingers up or catch balls above the waist with the fingers down.

Never catch a ball above the waist with the fingers down.

Glove not dirty When the glove is not down on a ground ball, many ground balls bounce under it.

FOOTWORK

Get in front A fielder who doesn't move to get in front of a ground ball will have difficulty making a clean fielding play. Only field grounders from the side when the ball is nearly out of reach.

Letting the ball play you A player backing up on a ground ball is asking for trouble. The player should play the hard-hit ball as it comes and move in on the slow rollers.

Back-pedaling Back-pedaling or trying to run backward toward a fly ball hit over a fielder's head is a great way to make an error. When the ball is hit way back, the fielder should turn and sprint toward the ball while watching it over her shoulder.

Keeping balanced A fielder must keep her balance as she receives the ball. Good balance provides a solid foundation for initiating accurate throws.

THROWING

Shuffle-stride The shuffle and stride when making a throw are parts of the throwing motion that lead to good accuracy. These movements should be smooth

The ball can easily be dropped when using a one-handed or swipe tag.

Never, *ever* turn your head when fielding a ball.

and powerful. Trying to throw off balance or throwing off the wrong foot can only lead to trouble.

Rushing When making a play, the fielder must get her feet set before attempting to throw. Rushed throws may go anywhere.

TAGS

High tags A high tag can allow a runner to slide under it to the base. As an umpire, I see this happen often. The glove should be low to make the runner slide into the tag.

Swipe or one-handed tags To properly make a tag, the ball should be grasped in the bare hand inside the glove. The ball can easily get out of the glove when a fielder tries a swipe or one-handed tag.

Most of these problems in fundamentals can be corrected with practice. When a player is warming up, playing catch, or in practice, she should be concentrating on the proper techniques of throwing and catching. With practice and repetition, the techniques and movements will become automatic.

15

FINAL THOUGHTS

Playing ball is fun. And there is a real sense of satisfaction in playing the game and doing it well. The sense of accomplishment is far more rewarding than records of team wins and losses. Softball is a team game, and it is most evident when examining a defense. There is beauty in seeing a team make plays as they should, with each player doing her part. Weak defensive teams can put on a very ugly show.

Without exception, the basic fundamentals of fielding and throwing apply to all positions. Any young player should learn to play as many different positions as possible. It can add to her value on a team. There will always be a place on a team for a fundamentally skilled player. Skill in playing doesn't just happen to a lucky few. It is acquired only after commitment, discipline, practice, and loads of hard work.

Playing the game well is a reward in itself and can lead to participation on all-star teams and traveling teams, making a high school team, and playing in college. Truly good players may be offered college scholarship help. All of these may be lofty goals at the outset, but these objectives are within reach for those players who really want to attain them and are willing to work hard.

ABOUT THE AUTHORS

During his thirty years of coaching at New Albany High School in Indiana, **Jacque Hunter** has received numerous coach of the year honors at the conference, district, and state levels. He has coached the state all-star team twice, and was inducted into the Indiana High School Coaches Hall of Fame in 2003. Coach Hunter's teams have won eleven sectional titles, seven regional titles, made six state finals appearances, were two times state runner-up, and won one Indiana State Championship. Many of Coach Hunter's players have continued their careers at the college level. He is coauthor of *A Guide for Young Softball Pitchers* and *A Young Softball Player's Guide to Hitting, Bunting, and Baserunning.*

Don Oster is a long-time baseball player and coach and is currently a high school and college softball umpire. He has managed a baseball team to the Little League World Series and was the pitching coach on four Babe Ruth World Series teams. Don is the author of *Large-*

mouth Bass and coauthor of *A Guide for Young Pitchers; A Guide for Young Batters and Base Runners; A Young Player's Guide to Fielding and Defense; A Guide for Young Softball Pitchers; A Young Softball Player's Guide to Hitting, Bunting, and Baserunning; Hunting Today's Whitetail;* and *Pronghorn Hunting.*